Also by Patrick Lencioni

Leadership Fables

The Five Temptations of a CEO

The Four Obsessions of an Extraordinary Executive

The Five Dysfunctions of a Team

Silos, Politics, and Turf Wars

Field Guide

Overcoming the Five Dysfunctions of a Team

Death *by* Meeting

A LEADERSHIP FABLE
. . . ABOUT SOLVING THE MOST
PAINFUL PROBLEM IN BUSINESS

Patrick Lencioni

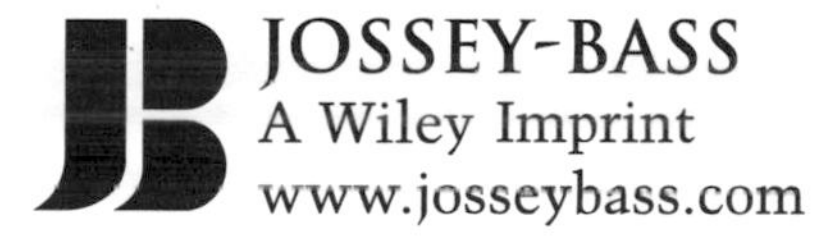

Published by Jossey-Bass
A Wiley Imprint
989 Market Street, San Francisco, CA 94103-1741 www.josseybass.com

Jossey-Bass books and products are available through most bookstores. To contact Jossey-Bass directly call our Customer Care Department within the U.S. at 800-956-7739, outside the U.S. at 317-572-3986, or fax 317-572-4002.

Jossey-Bass also publishes its books in a variety of electronic formats. Some content that appears in print may not be available in electronic books.

Library of Congress Cataloging-in-Publication Data

Lencioni, Patrick, 1965–
Death by meeting: a leadership fable about solving the most painful problem in business/by Patrick Lencioni.
p. cm.
ISBN 0-7879-6805-6 (alk. paper)
1. Business meetings. I. Title.
HF5734.5.L46 2004
658.4'56—dc22 2003026452

Printed in the United States of America
FIRST EDITION
HB Printing 10 9 8 7 6 5 4

CONTENTS

For my extraordinary wife, Laura,
for your unwavering confidence and optimism.

INTRODUCTION

"If I didn't have to go to meetings, I'd like my job a lot more."

It's a remark I've heard from many of the leaders I've worked with over the years. I used to think that it was understandable—even humorous—but I've come to the conclusion that it's actually a sad comment on the state of our business culture.

Imagine hearing a surgeon saying to a nurse before surgery: "If I didn't have to operate on people, I might actually like this job." Or a symphony conductor preparing for a performance: "If it weren't for these concerts, I would enjoy my work more." Or even a professional baseball player: "I'd love my job if I didn't have to play in these games."

Ridiculous, right? But that's exactly what we're doing when we lament our meetings.

Think about it this way. For those of us who lead and manage organizations, meetings are pretty much what we do. After all, we're not paid for doing anything exceedingly tangible or physical, like delivering babies or kicking field goals or doing stand-up comedy. Whether we like it or not, meetings are the closest thing to an operating room, a playing field, or a stage that we have.

And yet most of us hate them. We complain about, try to avoid, and long for the end of meetings, even when we're running the darn things! How pathetic is it that we have come to accept that the activity most central to the running of our organizations is inherently painful and unproductive?

All of this is an unnecessary shame because meetings are critical. They are where presidential cabinets discuss whether or not to go to war; where governors and their aides debate the merits of raising or lowering taxes; where CEOs and their staffs consider the decision to launch a brand, introduce a product, or close a factory.

And so my question is this: If we hate meetings, can we be making good decisions and successfully leading our organizations? I don't think so. There is simply no substitute for a good meeting—a dynamic, passionate, and focused engagement—when it comes to extracting the collective wisdom of a team. The hard truth is, bad meetings almost always lead to bad decisions, which is the best recipe for mediocrity.

But there is hope. By taking a contrarian, nontraditional view of meetings, and following a few specific guidelines that have nothing to do with video-conferencing, interactive software, or Robert's Rules of Order, we can transform what is now painful and tedious into something productive, compelling, and even energizing. In the process, we can also differentiate ourselves from our competitors who continue to waste time, energy, and enthusiasm lamenting the drudgery of meetings.

To illustrate how this can be accomplished, I've written a fictional story about an executive in a unique struggle with meetings. Following the story is a practical description of my suggestions for implementing these ideas in your organization.

Good luck as you work to make your meetings more effective, and restore some of the passion that you and your people deserve.

The Fable

PREVIEW

Casey McDaniel had never been so nervous in his life. Not when he was a sixteen-year-old preparing to speak at his father's funeral. Not before he proposed marriage to his wife. Not when he stood over a nine-foot putt that would win or lose the biggest golf tournament of his career.

No, this was the moment. In just ten minutes The Meeting would begin, and Casey had every reason to believe that his performance over the next two hours would determine the fate of his career, his financial future, and the company he had built from scratch. For a moment he thought he was going to be physically ill.

How could my life have unraveled so quickly? he wondered.

PART ONE

Flashback

THE MAN

Most of his employees would describe Casey as an extraordinary man—but just an ordinary CEO.

On a personal level, they genuinely liked their leader. Casey was a devoted husband, a loving father to his four children, a committed parishioner at Sacred Heart Church, and a helpful friend and neighbor. It was almost impossible not to like—even admire—the man.

Which made his limitation as a leader all the more mystifying.

HIS STORY

The McDaniel family had lived modestly in Carmel for the past fifty years, and Casey grew up on or around the many golf courses in the area, usually as a caddy or gardener. His affinity for golf was matched only by his love for computers, so he left home after high school to attend the University of Arizona on a golf scholarship, where he studied electrical engineering and computer science. Four years later he graduated toward the middle of his academic class, but at the top of the Pac-10 Conference in golf.

The lure of joining the PGA Tour, and someday playing back home at Pebble Beach in front of friends and family, was too much for Casey to resist. So he joined a qualifying tour where he quickly became one of the more popular players on the circuit with his quiet humor and generosity toward any fellow golfers who needed a little advice about their stroke.

Over the course of the next five years, Casey won a few more than his share of second-tier tournaments and earned enough money to keep his head far above water. But just as he was about to break through to the big tour, he developed a chronic case of what golfers call the yips—an almost clinical disorder that makes it difficult to remain steady while in the act of putting. Plenty of promising players had their careers cut short by the pseudo-psychological yips, and Casey reluctantly counted himself among them.

Never one to let disappointment keep him down for too long, Casey returned home with a new sense of purpose—and an idea. In a matter of months, he got married, bought a tiny bungalow with the earnings he had saved, hired two local programmers, and began hacking away at what he believed would be the most realistic golf video game that the market had ever seen.

The initial results would wildly exceed even his expectations.

BREAK

Within two years of launching his company, Yip Software, Casey released his first product, which immediately set the standard for realism in all sports-related games. Because of his in-depth background in the sport, the game reflected deep knowledge of many of the subtle aspects of actual golf venues, including of course, the putting greens.

Almost immediately the game became a favorite of the most important focus group of customers imaginable: golfers themselves.

Because he had become close friends with many players who were now on the tour, Casey was able to arrange inexpensive but effective sponsorship deals with a few of the better young players. But it was a purely accidental occurrence that propelled Yip's success beyond being a niche video game and onto the pages of *Sports Illustrated.*

One of Casey's friends won his first PGA tournament less than a year after the product had been released. During his post-tournament press conference, he was asked about the improvement in his putting. Almost embarrassed, he admitted, “I can’t believe I’m going to say this, but I think it may have something to do with a video game I’ve been playing lately. . . .”

And the cat was out of the bag.

THE RIDE

Almost immediately, serious golfers everywhere, many of whom hadn't played a video game in their lives, were calling Yip's 800 number to order a game. Casey quickly opened a small office, hired a dozen employees, and held on for dear life.

Before long, the game would be available in almost every pro shop and game store in the country. The next eight years of Casey's life would be an iterative exercise of hiring more people, programming new games, marketing to more stores, moving to larger offices. Not to mention having more kids.

By the tenth anniversary of the company (and his marriage), Casey and his wife, Patricia, were raising four children, and his company had brought eight successful games to market, covering golf, cycling, and most recently, tennis. Thanks to Casey's attention to detail, the games consistently gained notoriety for their accurate depiction of real-life venues around the world, from the links at St. Andrews in Scotland to the hills of the Pyrenees Mountains in the Tour de France to the grass courts at Wimbledon.

From the beginning, Casey refused to produce violent, fantasy-oriented games aimed at kids. Instead, he insisted that Yip's products be focused on sports, and always realistic and innovative. As a result, Yip developed a strong following among adults and older teens who considered themselves relatively serious athletes.

More than the brand he had built, however, Casey was proudest of the fact that he employed almost two hundred people, many of whom had grown up with the company. And he couldn't deny the pride he took in his headquarters site, a beautifully renovated historic building in Old Monterey.

On a local level, Yip had become a shining star in the community, providing more professional jobs than any non-industrial venture in the area other than the famed aquarium. Casey had transformed an idea into a niche company that was the darling of his hometown, not to mention an unqualified success story in the industry.

But like so many success stories, there was another side to Yip and its CEO. And it was as baffling as it was undeniable.

MEDIOCRITY

Even Casey's biggest supporters, and he had many, would privately concede that Yip Software might have been twice its current size under the stewardship of a more focused and disciplined leader.

It wasn't that Casey was incompetent or uninterested in business. In fact, he had an extraordinary knack for sensing what customers were looking for and tweaking products to meet their needs long before his competitors realized what was happening. As a result, Casey had developed a reputation for understanding his market as well as any analyst, journalist, or executive in the industry.

In theory, the company's results should have spoken for themselves. Yip had never failed to make a profit and had consistently garnered awards for its products. To the naked eye, Casey and his company looked like a driven, determined enterprise.

But in reality, the firm was something of an under-achiever. And it started with Casey, who seemed to be just as satisfied with squeaking out a win by a narrow margin as he was with scoring a decisive victory. If the numbers added up at the end of each quarter, and he was able to squeeze in a few rounds of golf every week, Casey was content—even happy.

His employees, however, were merely satisfied. Even complacent. They had grown accustomed to the fact that the company would somehow find a way to hit its targets, meet its payroll, and have just enough cushion left over at the end of each year for modest annual raises and a grand summer picnic. No one ever seemed to worry about Yip's fate.

But something was definitely missing. For a company that made popular, state-of-the-art video games in a beautiful place like Monterey, California, there was a surprising lack of excitement among the people who worked there. And if anyone doubted this, they would only have to observe five minutes of the Yip executives' weekly staff meeting.

THE RITUAL

Lethargic. Unfocused. Passionless. Those were the most common words that visitors used to describe what they witnessed after attending even part of an executive staff meeting.

The Yip executive team was painfully aware of their tedious weekly ritual. But they decided long ago that it was an innocuous problem, one of the necessary evils of doing business. Besides, they reasoned, every other company's meetings were probably just as bad.

But they had underestimated the magnitude of the problem. It certainly never occurred to them that the company's culture would come to mirror those meetings.

MALAISE

Unlike their aggressive competitors, Yip employees almost never felt compelled to stay at the office into the evening or come in on weekends, and they didn't talk much about work outside the walls of the company. Among rank-and-file employees, competitive information or industry news rarely found its way into hallway discussions, seemingly nudged out by more relevant topics, like television, youth soccer, and coastal fog.

Whenever employees ventured away from Monterey to attend a trade show or industry conference, they always came home fascinated by the passion that customers and distributors felt for Yip's products, and how much this contrasted with the attitude of Yip's own employees.

Even new hires were surprised about the lack of passion they encountered after joining the company. But like their co-workers, they quickly learned to accept that Yip was never going to realize the full potential that its products deserved because of what they would describe as the subtle mediocrity that pervaded the organization.

And yet, in spite of all this, people rarely left the company. After all, their leader was an exceedingly good man, and not as bad an executive as many of the other CEOs they had worked for. Besides, where else would they go? There were no better job opportunities in the tourism-dominated coastal community.

Even the most ambitious employees had learned to accept their situation because they couldn't imagine living anywhere else. As long as Casey was the sole owner of Yip, that was just the way things would be.

But things have a way of changing.

PART TWO

Plot Point

FIRST DOMINO

There was never any doubt among the executives that employee morale was a little lower than they would have liked. But it was never bad enough, in their opinion, to warrant much attention.

Until the day Casey hired the company's first vice president of human resources, Michelle Hannah. Within weeks of joining the firm, Michelle conducted an employee survey to get a sense of her new company. The data she received indicated that morale was indeed lower than in other organizations where she had worked, and more important, that employees throughout Yip "seemed largely unconcerned about the business," as she described them.

Strangely, Michelle's presentation awakened and unnerved the executives a little. Somehow, having real data about a problem that everyone already knew existed gave them greater cause for concern. And while no one had ever seemed interested in addressing the issue before, suddenly they all had strong opinions about it.

Matt McKenna, the skeptical head of product development and the technical brains behind Yip's games for the past seven years, speculated that employees were frustrated by the organization's never-ending pursuit of new products and features. "I think people would just like to stick with one thing for a while, and focus on quality," he pleaded, in a way that suggested the complaint was his own, not that of employees at large.

Sophia Nikolas, Yip's VP of sales, had a completely different take on the situation. With her customary enthusiasm, she made a pitch to the team that they had heard many times before. "I know we've always been against this, but maybe we need to reconsider our decision not to do fantasy and adventure games for kids. I'm out there every day, and that's where the market's growing fastest."

Casey shook his head and thought out loud. "I think our people just need something to rally around. A new goal or a challenge." A few heads began to nod, and it seemed that Casey had come closest to identifying the issue. Unfortunately, before anyone could confirm their CEO's insight, the next opinion was on the table.

It came from Tim Carter, Yip's unsophisticated and outspoken CFO. As usual, he was more ardent in his theory than his peers, and his declaration had a financial spin to it. "Listen, our employees have been watching our products win awards for almost a decade now. I think they're wondering where the financial upside is."

No one wanted to comment on Tim's remark, both because they weren't convinced he was right, and because they knew how sensitive a subject it had become over the past few years, especially for Casey.

And then Connor Michaels, Yip's jovial head of marketing and sports research, nodded his head just slightly, causing the room to look his way. Casually, he admitted that he shared some of Tim's sentiments, but kindly joked that he had come to accept what he called "his fate."

While each theory struck a chord in him, it was Connor's comment that kept Casey awake that night. Though he had never really been motivated by money, Casey took pride in the notion that he was helping employees pay their mortgages, go on nice vacations, pay their children's tuition, and contribute to worthy charities. The idea that they might be feeling under-rewarded was a painful pill for him to swallow, and he couldn't deny that any responsibility for unrealized potential at Yip fell squarely on his shoulders.

MISDIAGNOSIS

Until that moment, Casey had always justified the apparent complacency of his employees as a desire to have balance in their lives. For the first time since founding the company, however, he wondered if he had simply been letting them down.

After initially deciding to dismiss the concern, Casey found himself increasingly distracted by it. Whenever he encountered someone who seemed less than enthusiastic about work, he couldn't help but wonder if they had lost interest because of the financial issues that Tim and Connor mentioned. Casey gradually came to the conclusion that something had to be done.

And so, on the night of Yip's tenth anniversary, Casey rented a local restaurant on Cannery Row for a company celebration. After dinner he toasted his employees and made an announcement he would soon regret: he was going to take the company public.

Overriding his fears, Casey decided it was time to give his people the financial payoff they deserved. Unfortunately, when Casey announced that he was going to do something, he almost always found a way to get it done.

MIRAGE

Casey and Tim immediately made arrangements to meet with bankers to begin laying the foundations for an initial public offering. It was something that Casey had vowed he would never do, not wanting to subject himself to the whims of a formal board of directors, and more importantly, "the street." But now he felt that he somehow owed it to his loyal employees. "And maybe I need a new challenge," he unconvincingly reasoned with himself.

And then, after a few weeks of reluctant planning, Casey stumbled on an opportunity that he suspected was too good to be true. He should have trusted his instincts.

The call came from J.T. Harrison, head of business development at Playsoft, the nation's second-largest maker of video games. The San Jose–based company had been built on more traditional video games targeted at kids, and was underrepresented in the sports market. As their target customers began to age, it seemed wise to consider moving into a category that might appeal to the buyers they liked to refer to as "older kids." And that's where Yip came into play.

Initial research by Harrison's team at Playsoft indicated that Casey McDaniel's company was an underperformer, especially considering the superior technology it had. That would make it the perfect acquisition vehicle for getting into the sports market quickly and cheaply, without having to spend two years in product development. If they could just improve Yip's performance, it was a chance for a home run.

Though Casey didn't like the idea of being part of one of the typical game companies, he decided to entertain the idea of selling Yip to Playsoft. But only on three conditions: he would continue to run his company autonomously, he would retain his entire management team, and he would be allowed to keep the Yip name as a separate, wholesome, sports-oriented brand.

If Playsoft's CEO, Wade Justin, would agree to those terms, Casey decided it would be a great opportunity to give his people the financial upside they deserved, without losing control of the company he had built. And besides, it would allow him to avoid the risk and stress that going public would entail. "The best of both worlds," was how he explained it to his wife the day he submitted the offer to J.T. Harrison. "But they aren't going to like it."

Surprisingly, Playsoft's executive team immediately agreed to the conditions. Wade Justin personally assured Casey that his company knew little about the sports game market and would not want to interfere with an already successful brand. He explained that several other divisions within Playsoft had almost complete autonomy and separate brand identities.

And so, within just weeks of the initial proposal, the deal was closed. Casey would receive, and distribute among his employees based on their time with the company, hundreds of thousands of shares of Playsoft stock, which they could sell after an initial six-month holding period.

He could not have imagined how little gratitude they would be feeling toward him when that time came.

ALARM

For the first few weeks after the acquisition, Yip employees bordered on giddy. Though nothing had really changed in their daily routines, their newfound paper wealth did wonders for morale. And while many of the old-timers were certainly enjoying the idea of shopping for new homes or cars, more than anything they felt a sense of validation that their patience had finally paid off.

And then something happened that changed everything.

Casey would never forget where he was and what he was doing when he heard the news. His CFO, Tim Carter, came by his office early one morning while he was talking to his real estate agent. Tim looked like he was about to be sick, so Casey abruptly ended his call.

Before Tim could speak, Casey commanded, "Shut the door."

Then Tim began. "You haven't logged on yet this morning have you?" It was more of a statement than a question, because Tim knew that if his boss had logged on, he would look sick too.

Casey braced himself. “No, why? What’s going on? Another terrorist attack?”

“No, nothing like that, thank God.”

A sigh of relief from Casey. “Oh, you had me scared.”

Tim continued. “The market’s down more than 12 percent since the opening bell.”

“What about—”

Before he could finish the sentence, Tim answered the question. “Playsoft’s down almost nine.”

“Well at least we’re doing better than. . . . ”

“Nine *points,*” Tim explained.

Casey looked almost sick. “This is bad.”

Little did he know.

SECOND DOMINO

Over the course of the next three weeks the market, and Playsoft's stock price, continued to slide. The mood in the office dropped lower than it had been in years. Casey was torn between two emotions: disappointment in himself for selling the company, and anger at the Playsoft executive team for not managing their business better. But he was a fair man and couldn't deny that the market collapse could not have been foreseen, and that no one in particular was to blame. He only hoped his employees would see it that way.

When he finally received a call from J.T. Harrison, Casey expected a conciliatory tone from the man that had brokered the suddenly ill-advised deal. He had already decided to be gracious with Harrison, and assure him that he could hardly blame him for such an unexpected turn of events.

Which is why he was surprised by Harrison's almost callous comments, and his subsequent request. "Yeah, it's a shame about the market. Live by the sword, die by the sword, I guess. Anyway, I'd like to come out and see you next week."

This was the first real interaction between the two since the acquisition closed, so Casey was curious as to the nature of the proposed visit. "What's up?"

"Nothing. I just thought I'd drop by and sit in on your next staff meeting, if that's okay. Get a little more acquainted with what's going on out there."

Caught off guard, Casey tried not to sound defensive. "Well, sure, if you want to. But I'm afraid you're not going to learn anything particularly interesting. Why don't you and I get together and we can talk about whatever you'd like to know."

If J.T. sensed any of Casey's discomfort, he didn't acknowledge it. "No, I'd rather come to the meeting, if that's alright." He wasn't asking.

"Okay then, we start at ten in the morning, on Monday. We usually go until—"

J.T. interrupted. "Hey, my other line's ringing. I'll see you next week."

And he was gone. At that moment Casey could have sworn he heard the first faint sounds of his world falling apart.

THE INVASION

On Monday morning Casey found himself uneasy about going to work, and he knew it had to do with J.T. Harrison's visit. And so he was less than pleased to see his guest sitting in his office when he arrived at ten minutes to ten.

J.T. was looking out the window toward the coastline. "It's so beautiful over here."

Casey felt as though he were entertaining a foreign invader, but he remained gracious. "You should come over more often. It's a great change of scenery." *Okay,* he decided. *That was too gracious.*

"I wish I had time." After a brief and shallow conversation about how busy they were, it was time to go to the staff meeting.

Only half of the team was in the conference room by ten, and though this was not unusual, it made Casey a little nervous given the presence of his special visitor. But within five minutes or so everyone who would be attending the meeting was seated and ready to go. Two members of the team, Matt and Michelle, had other commitments of some kind.

Casey began the meeting as he usually did, by confirming that they had all received copies of the minutes from the previous meeting, and then humorously chiding everyone for not sending him any suggestions for the agenda. He then passed out the agenda he had put together on his own, which included five items: expense policy, strategic planning, management training, stock reporting, and competitive update.

Casey teed up the first topic by announcing, "There are two issues that we need to talk about relative to expenses." He then turned to his CFO. "Go ahead, Tim."

"First, we have to get variable costs under control. We also have to get our expenses done sooner, and change our forms to better align with Playsoft's." Tim looked to their visitor to acknowledge the parent company.

For the next hour, the group patiently and dispassionately discussed expense reports, expense policies, and anything else that had to do with the administration of expenses. J.T. seemed to have tuned out altogether, which was frankly something of a relief to Casey.

Finally, as the conversation lost whatever steam it ever had, Casey decided, "Okay, that's enough on expenses." He looked at his agenda, "Let's talk about the strategic plan."

J.T. seemed to come out of his trance, suddenly energized by the possibility of an interesting discussion.

"Why don't you tell us where the planning process is right now, Connor?" Casey liked to involve his people as much as possible at these meetings.

Connor gave a ten-minute update on what had been accomplished in terms of industry data collection and preliminary research. He then laid out, using colorful slides with sound effects, the time line for developing the company's strategic plan for the upcoming year.

At one point, Sophia asked Connor and Casey to share their thoughts on what the general direction of the plan might be. "Or maybe you can just tell us the key issues that we'll need to discuss."

What commenced was a forty-minute discussion, certainly more interesting than the last one, about competitive pressures and market trends. But while there was little doubt that Casey and his team had a grasp of the issues they faced, J.T. decided there was something missing. It was passion. And urgency. *These people sound like they're discussing a case study about someone else's business rather than their own company's future.*

With just ten minutes remaining in the two-hour meeting, Casey brought that discussion to a halt. "Okay, we'll have plenty of time to talk about the strategic plan in the months ahead. We've got a few other issues to cover today."

As he surveyed his list, Sophia spoke up. "I was hoping we could talk about increasing magazine advertising next quarter."

Connor responded before Casey could. "I thought we agreed on the placements last week."

"I guess we did, but I wasn't really comfortable with what we decided. And when I talked to my people about it, they said we need to ramp up a little in trade magazines if we want to get some momentum heading into Christmas."

Casey sighed and looked to Tim. "Is there anything we can do with our budget to shift costs next quarter?"

"I'll see, but I want to make sure we really need to do this. I don't want us coming up short in November."

Casey agreed. "Our competitors are going to go crazy this holiday season, and we don't want to spend our money too early."

Connor weighed in, frustrated, but not at the head of sales. "True, but Sophia might be right. If we can get momentum before they do, it could make our Christmas spend that much more effective. And theirs might be neutralized. I just wish we'd thought about this a month ago, or even last week."

J.T. knew little about Yip's business. But he was sure that this was the only animated conversation of the past two hours. Unfortunately, it was about to end.

Casey intervened. "Okay, we have five minutes left, and we haven't even talked about management training, stock reporting or competitive analysis." He paused for a moment. "Tim, give us a thirty-second overview on the stock situation."

"Alright, basically we, as officers of the company, cannot sell our stock—not that we'd want to at this point—until the Playsoft books are closed and the numbers are released. And that goes for any employees who have material knowledge of our revenue. So let's keep me informed about anyone on your staffs who should be considered insiders. I don't have to remind you all about the cost of doing this wrong. The SEC isn't feeling too generous right now."

More than one of the people sitting around the table had questions for Tim, but none dared ask them so close to the end of the meeting.

Casey continued, aware of the group's desperation for getting out of the meeting on time. "Michelle couldn't be here today, but she asked me to tell you all that she's scheduling the management training for the first week of October. Everyone who manages people or who has a manager title will be expected to attend the full three-day seminar."

Again, in spite of their many questions and objections, no one bothered to say anything. Two and a half minutes to go.

Finally, "Okay, what's the competitive report look like, Connor, Sophia?" The respective heads of marketing and sales looked at one another as if to say, "Where should we start?" Sophia went first.

"We just heard through the grapevine that GoBox and Gamestar will be releasing new golf games later this year."

Connor added, "They're trying to establish themselves in the market as the irreverent player in our space. They want to portray us as being stodgy and targeted at old folks, so they can take advantage of all the kids who are into golf because of Tiger Woods."

"So what do we do?" asked Tim.

Casey looked at his watch. "We talk about it next time. It's noon and Sophia and I have a phone call with Wal-Mart at two o'clock central time, if I remember correctly." Sophia nodded. And just like that, the meeting was over and people scattered like antsy fourth-graders headed for recess.

J.T. watched them leave, amazed.

INTERPRETATION

Though he could not put his finger on what he had just witnessed, J.T. decided there was something almost impressive about it. That these undeniably competent executives could sit through two hours of mind-numbing conversation, touching occasionally on interesting topics and then letting them drift away, was one thing. But to do that without the slightest appearance of frustration was another matter entirely.

What J.T. did not know was that the Yip executive team had long ago resigned themselves to dealing with their horrible meetings. Important decisions—and the discussions that led to them—usually took place in Casey's office, involving him and one or two other executives, depending on the issue.

Unfortunately for Casey, it was only in those sessions that one could really observe his remarkable intuition and judgment.

Certainly not during meetings. Those were mere formalities. And painful ones. Tedious, wandering affairs, covering anything and everything under the sun. Expense policies.

Marketing strategy. Office supplies. Vacation schedules. Technology trends. Facilities. Every topic was fair game. And none ever seemed to get resolved completely, at least not until Casey later held court in his office.

Interestingly, as awful as the meetings were, they never, ever went beyond their scheduled end time. Regardless of how many agenda items had yet to be discussed, Casey concluded the sessions at twelve o'clock sharp, without a complaint from anyone. And he was particularly proud of this, especially after years of watching meetings run overtime to the dissatisfaction of his executives.

Still, punctuality notwithstanding, it was no surprise that any excuse to miss the weekly meeting was welcomed by Casey's team. In fact, it was somewhat rare that all six executives were present for the entire "staff infection," as the sessions jokingly came to be known.

But the meetings were not a joke when it came to their impact on Casey's company. They were the birthplace of the morale problems at Yip, the single point from which confusion, dispassion, and ultimately, lethargy emanated throughout the organization. All issues were eventually considered there, and by the end of the weekly ritual, they had been drained of their energy and momentum.

There was no doubt that Casey and his team had misjudged the danger posed by their meetings. And that was before they knew anything about what J.T. Harrison was up to.

J.T.

Direct, abrupt, almost cold at times, J.T. Harrison never seemed frazzled or challenged. In just seven years, he had risen from a marketing manager to his current position as executive vice president of business development. Which meant that among his various responsibilities, J.T. did deals.

It was in this capacity, handling mergers and acquisitions, that Harrison had established a legendary, though somewhat murky, reputation throughout the industry.

Playsoft's competitors feared the man, who would often represent the company in lawsuits and negotiations. His staff worked like dogs for him, late at night and on weekends, though no one outside the department ever heard them complain. Most surprising of all, his peers claimed to like J.T., though employees around the company decided that they were merely afraid to speak ill of a man who someday could be their boss.

As well known as he had become, few people inside or outside Playsoft would say that they really knew J.T. Harrison. Which was fine with him. His reputation alone had been enough to intimidate the right people on the outside, and drive the right people on the inside.

Casey would soon learn more about the man than he wanted to know.

FIRST SHOTS

The call came late the next week, but not from Harrison. That would have been better. It was one of his young MBAs. "Hello, Mr. McDaniel, I'm Tony from Business Development at Playsoft. I'm calling on behalf of J.T. Harrison to set up a series of meetings, or sessions, I guess, over the next three months."

Casey didn't know what to say. "Excuse me? Who are you?"

The MBA was unflappable. "Tony, from Playsoft. I work for J.T. Harrison in Business—"

Out of character, Casey interrupted. "Right, I got that. What is it that you want?"

"I'm not exactly sure. All I know is that J.T. wanted me to let you know that he will be coming to some of your staff meetings for the rest of the summer, until September 15th, it looks like. He'll try to let you know in advance, but sometimes he might just pop in."

A long and awkward silence was finally broken by Casey, who was trying to be calm. "And what is the purpose of this?" Before Tony could answer, Casey continued. "Do you think that maybe J.T. and I ought to talk about this directly?" Again, he didn't wait for an answer. "I'm sorry, Tom."

"That's Tony."

"Right. Tony. I'm sorry, but I'll talk to J.T. about this myself. Please have him call me when he gets a chance."

"Will do, Mr. McDaniel."

"Call me Casey."

"Sure. And I'm looking forward to meeting you when I get a chance to come over to Monterey myself."

Casey wanted to reach through the phone and strangle the youngster on the other end, but knew that it was Harrison who needed strangling. So he summoned every bit of courtesy he could, and said, "That would be great. Thanks, Tony." And he hung up wondering what else would go wrong that day.

He would find out five minutes later when his assistant, Gia Belli, came into his office.

WHEN IT RAINS

"I'm pregnant!" she announced joyfully to her boss of eight years.

Casey came out from behind his desk and hugged his assistant, something he rarely did with anyone at work. Though he had been distracted by his problems with J.T. Harrison, he made every effort to demonstrate to his assistant that he was as happy as she was. After all, he and Patricia had been hoping and praying for Gia and her husband, who had been trying to have children for the past five years. Why not be happy?

And then Gia dropped the bomb. She explained that she was actually four months along in her pregnancy, and that she hadn't said anything yet because she was worried about losing the babies.

"Babies?" Casey asked.

"Twins!" she announced. "The doctors said it will be a high-risk pregnancy, given all the trouble we've had getting pregnant. And that means," she hesitated before delivering the final blow, "I have to stop working in two weeks. I'll probably be on complete bed rest within a month." She winced, hoping her boss wouldn't be upset.

True to his character, in that particular moment Casey showed nothing but reassurance and excitement for Gia. But later that night he would confess to his wife that the first thought that crossed his mind was, "What am I going to do about replacing her?"

It wasn't that Gia had been one of those extraordinary assistants who sees around corners and knows the business as well as anyone else in the firm. In fact, Casey had often wondered what it would be like to have a hungrier, savvier administrative person running his office. But Gia was a loyal, pleasant, and steady presence in Casey's life, and this was a time when he welcomed anything steady.

"Maybe I could get by for a while without an assistant," Casey remarked to Patricia later that night, looking for her response.

"Right," Patricia responded sarcastically. "That's exactly what you need. More administrative things to do. You might as well just call J.T. Harrison and offer him your job. Come on, Casey, you have to find someone to fill in for her."

Casey knew she was right. "I'll have her call the temporary agency tomorrow so I can start interviewing people next week."

Patricia was quiet now, and Casey could tell she was coming up with a new idea. And since most of her ideas turned out to be good ones, he prodded her. "What are you thinking?"

"Well, maybe you should consider bringing in a different kind of admin for a while. Someone who can add value in different ways. Someone who doesn't mind doing what Gia does, but with more energy. Maybe she would give you a different perspective."

Casey thought about it, but before he could respond, one of his younger girls was calling him from the next room. He was off to get her a glass of water, and the conversation drifted away. But he would not forget his wife's idea.

SERENDIPITY

Two days later Casey received an e-mail message from Ken Petersen, an old family friend and golf coach who years ago had moved over the hills to the Bay Area, where he now coached high school basketball. Ken had become something of a father figure back when Casey's dad passed away, and they had stayed close ever since.

Ken was writing to say that he and his wife, Kathryn, were coming over to Monterey to play golf, and they were hoping to have dinner with Casey and Patricia. Casey initially decided to decline the invitation to avoid having to recount the entire sordid tale of Yip and Playsoft and the stock price and J.T. Harrison. Then his wife called.

"Hey, I just talked to Kathryn, and I thought we could take her and Ken to that new Mexican restaurant tomorrow night."

Patricia loved Kathryn and Ken as much as her husband did, and Casey knew that it would be difficult to get out of the date. He explained his lack of enthusiasm for seeing old friends at this point in his career, but his wife wouldn't hear it.

"Come on, Casey. Don't be a wuss. Besides, this is exactly when you need to see old friends the most. Anyway, it'll be fun, and you need a break."

Casey reluctantly agreed to the date, not knowing how valuable Patricia's guidance would turn out to be.

THE REFERRAL

Most of the dinner with the Petersens was exactly what Casey needed. Talking about something other than work allowed him to relax and put life in perspective. Until dessert.

It was then that Kathryn asked about the company.

Casey couldn't blame her. After all, she had recently retired after fifteen years at the Bay Area's only automotive joint venture where she eventually ran operations. Kathryn was now in-between careers and restlessly spending more time at home. Her interest in Yip was born out of genuine concern for Casey, as well as the need to get her intellectual feet wet, if only for the evening. So Casey obliged.

He explained the entire situation to her. His rationale for selling the company to Playsoft. His disappointment at what had happened to the stock price, and to morale. And even his fears about one particular, unnamed executive from corporate.

Kathryn restrained herself from offering any prescriptive advice, short of encouraging Casey to let go of his guilt about employees. "Come on now. Your employees have done very well for themselves, and I happen to know some of the extraordinary gestures you've made to them over the years. You have nothing to apologize for. Besides, they're adults and they understand how business works."

Casey couldn't deny that he appreciated hearing what Kathryn had to say.

And then she surprised Casey with an anecdote about someone at Playsoft. "An old acquaintance of mine once worked on a deal with those guys. His company sold them an obscure piece of technology, I think. Anyway, I don't know how it all turned out because I've lost touch with my friend. But I do remember him saying that he wanted to strangle some guy named J.R. something."

"J.T. Harrison," Casey corrected her.

"That's right. J.T. Harrison." Kathryn was excited that Casey knew who she was talking about. "He's a piece of work, I guess. Do you know him?"

Casey nodded painfully, and explained that this was the guy from corporate he had mentioned earlier.

Patricia saw her husband sliding again, and quickly changed the subject. "Hey, you don't know any great administrative assistants who need a temporary job, do you? Casey's admin, Gia, is having twins and won't be back until next year."

Kathryn turned to her husband, and pleaded with him jokingly. "Oh, let me take the job. Please. It would be so much fun." They all laughed at Kathryn's distaste for retirement.

"Oh yeah, that's all I need." Casey complained humorously. "You'd have my job in two weeks."

Ken suddenly had an idea, which he announced to no one in particular. "Hey, you know who would be great for this job? Will."

Patricia seemed confused. "You mean your little boy?"

Kathryn laughed. "Our little boy is twenty-seven years old."

Ken explained his son's situation. "Will's taking some time off after finishing graduate school, to figure life out. He needs to make a little money, though, so it might be perfect."

Casey looked at Kathryn for her assessment. She had been caught off guard and seemed to be processing the idea right there. "I don't know. I mean, he certainly understands the basics of business. He practically went through b-school with me when I was studying at night, and he listened to me talk about work every night at dinner."

Ken continued. "Listen, Kathryn doesn't like to say it, but I don't mind. Will is brilliant. And he works like a dog."

"What exactly do you mean when you say brilliant?" Casey wanted to know.

Ken gladly bragged about his son. "Well, he tested off the charts for analytical ability in grad school."

"But it's more than that," Kathryn explained. "It's difficult to describe, but Will has this way of understanding and explaining things a little differently than most people. He seems to be able to create order out of chaos, regardless of what he's doing. I wish I could say it was genetic, but I'm afraid I have no idea where he gets it."

Ken jumped in again. "Even as a kid he was like that. He reorganized the garage when he was five. And he invented a new offense for my high school basketball team when he was in junior high." He laughed. "I still use that offense today."

Casey was certainly curious now. "What did he study?"

Kathryn answered, "Film and television in grad school. As an undergrad he majored in psychology and business, spent some time in advertising, and then was determined to go into psychotherapy. He was a year into his Ph.D. program, and doing extremely well—"

Ken interrupted. "When suddenly he decided he wanted to be a Hollywood director, so he went to USC and got his master's in film." He rolled his eyes playfully to indicate his mild disappointment with his son's fickle career change and never-ending educational pursuits. "Now he's not sure if he's more interested in the business or creative side of things. But I think he'll end up in production. He really seems to enjoy media and technology."

Casey liked that.

"Anyway," Kathryn explained, "he's out of money and needs some time off to catch his breath, maybe do some writing, before diving into Hollywood head first. So he's definitely available."

The conversation had moved away from conjecture, so Patricia called the question. "Well, what do you think?" She was directing the comment as much at Kathryn and Ken as her husband.

Kathryn shrugged her shoulders. "Well, he's certainly overqualified for the job. But given his situation, he might be happy to do it for a while." She laughed. "And if it works out, he'll be the best temporary assistant you've ever had."

Ken nodded his agreement.

Patricia closed the deal. "Why not, Casey? And you don't have to feel guilty about letting him go when Gia comes back."

Casey smiled at his wife, shrugged and said to his friends, "Have Will call me sometime next week—if he's interested. He might not be, you know."

They all agreed, and Casey decided there was a good chance he would never hear from Will. He was wrong.

PART THREE

Protagonist

WILL POWER

When Casey arrived on Monday, there was a note on his desk from Gia.

Will Petersen called. I set up an interview for three o'clock this afternoon.

Casey immediately walked to Gia's cubicle, and asked to see Will's résumé.

"He's going to e-mail it to me in a few minutes. I'll give you a copy as soon as I get it."

Casey thanked her, turned to leave, and then caught himself. "Oh, I haven't seen Will in years. What's he like?"

"You mean on the phone?"

Casey nodded.

"He was nice. In fact, he was really nice. I can't wait to meet him."

Casey spent most of the day holed up in a conference room with Sophia, Connor, and members of their staffs talking about competitive positioning and branding. Before he knew it, Gia was standing at the door waving a résumé in her hand.

Excusing himself from the marathon working session, Casey walked with Gia toward his office, where Will was waiting. Casey glanced at the résumé as he walked. "Anything I should know about him?" he asked his assistant.

"No. But he doesn't *look* like an administrative assistant."

Casey laughed. "What's that supposed to mean?"

Before Gia could explain, the discussion came to an end as they reached the office and Will Petersen.

On first glance, there was nothing remarkable about Will. He was neither tall nor short. He was certainly not heavy, but not particularly thin either. His hair was light-colored, but not enough to be considered blond. Will Petersen was one of those people the police would have a hard time describing on television if he escaped from prison or committed a crime.

But anything nondescript about Will disappeared as soon as he engaged with someone. As his dad liked to say, he was "as likably confident a kid as there is in the world." Everyone who knew him said there was something intensely magnetic about Will.

"Hello, Mr. McDaniel. Thanks for seeing me today."

As soon as Casey shook hands with Will he had a sense he would hire him. "Come on, Will, call me Casey, and it's great to see you again. I think it's been almost ten years since I watched you play ball in high school."

Will seemed slightly embarrassed. "Yeah, I was the only power forward on the court under six feet tall."

"And you out-rebounded every other kid in the gym, if I remember right. Your dad said you were the hardest worker he ever coached."

"Well, when you're not naturally gifted. . . ."

Casey dismissed Will's modesty. "You're a lot like your dad. Has he ever told you how we became friends?"

"He just said that he helped you during a tough time, and that you're one of his favorite people in the world."

Casey was embarrassed by the compliment.

Will continued. "And if you know my dad, you know he doesn't usually say things like that."

Sufficiently uncomfortable with the flattery, Casey changed the subject. The tone of the conversation suddenly shifted toward an interview, albeit a friendly one. "So, Will, tell me what you've been up to lately, and why I should hire you."

"How much did my parents tell you?"

"Not that much, actually. Just that you studied film and television down at USC. And that you know something about business."

Will seemed slightly relieved by Casey's answer, and dove right in. "Okay. That's right. I've been down south getting my master's degree in film and media studies, and I'm trying to decide if I want to be on the creative or business end of things. Before film school I spent a year studying psychology at the graduate level. And before that I worked for three years with an advertising agency in the city, doing everything from television and radio grunt work to running the creative department for their retail clients."

"It sounds like you were promoted a few times."

Will nodded, and quickly brought the conversation back to Casey's original question. "As far as why you should hire me, well, I'm not exactly sure. When I started working at the advertising agency, I did a few months of administrative work for the managing partner. He said I gave him better advice than the consultants he paid $500 an hour."

Both of them laughed.

"Well, first of all, I'm not concerned about you being qualified. You're immensely overqualified. And that's the problem. Are you sure you want to do this?"

Will smiled. "Well, it's certainly not my calling in life, if that's what you mean. But after four years of graduate school, I need a break. And the prospect of spending some time living with a buddy of mine in Carmel, working a little, playing some golf, getting in shape, doing some writing—that seems pretty good to me."

Casey was intrigued. "Sounds good to me too. Maybe I should take the job instead of you."

They laughed again. "But I should tell you that the next few months might be a little busier than usual, so you might not get as much golf or writing time as you'd like right away. We're in the middle of an integration. You know about the Playsoft acquisition, right?"

"Yeah, and that it's been tough going since then, at least in terms of the stock price." Will hoped he didn't make Casey feel too bad, but he could have sworn he saw him cringe for a nanosecond.

"And that's why this is such a critical time. In addition to introducing new products, we'll probably need to find a way to squeeze more revenue out of our current products, not to mention getting our act together as a company."

Will already felt comfortable enough to press Casey a little. "What do you mean by 'getting your act together'?"

"Well," Casey looked out the window. "I just think we'll be under a little more scrutiny than we'd like. I have a feeling Playsoft is going to be watching expenses for a while."

Will detected a hint of evasiveness, but decided to let that one go. "So how can I help you?"

Casey didn't have an answer ready. "I don't know. I suppose if you can keep things moving until Gia comes back, that would be a good start. And given your non-traditional background, don't hesitate to dive into something that might not sound like a typical part of an admin's job."

Will would always remember that interview for two reasons. First, he could not have imagined how fateful Casey's last comment would quickly become. Second, there was something Will had decided not to mention to his new boss, something that would make the next several months more interesting than he might have liked.

DISORDER

Until the age of fourteen, Will had been a difficult kid. In spite of what seemed like a generally sensitive and kind personality, he always managed to create problems for teachers, coaches, and other students. And it usually centered around inappropriate remarks and rude comments that Will made in particularly sensitive situations, seemingly out of the blue.

Though his parents, older brothers, and closest friends had come to accept this strange and unpleasant aspect of Will, he suffered because of it. Poor grades. No interest from girls. More than his share of fist-fights.

And then one day an English teacher at St. Jude's High School asked Will to come by his house after school to see his wife, who was a psychiatrist. After just an hour, she diagnosed Will as having some kind of psychological disorder. He was too socially adept, she said, to be behaving the way her husband had described him. And though she had not seen Will's exact symptoms before, she believed he had a mild version of something like Obsessive-Compulsive Disorder or Tourette's Syndrome. Or both.

Fortunately, Will's problem was not so severe that it rendered him helpless. Unfortunately, however, his case was just moderate enough not to warrant an early diagnosis as a child. He would be forever grateful to that teacher who had learned enough about his wife's work to know that Will probably wasn't just a disagreeable kid, but had a clinical medical problem.

Like most people afflicted with similar disorders, Will was aware of the inappropriateness of his comments but seemed completely unable to restrain himself. He did, however, seem to find welcome relief in three particular situations: when he was engaged in playing a sport, when he was engrossed in a film, and when he distracted himself during class by taking notes. So Will played plenty of basketball, saw every movie he could, and took copious notes.

From the moment Will's parents received the call from the psychiatrist who diagnosed their son, they were beside themselves with relief, for two reasons. First, they could finally attribute his struggle to a cause other than an irascible personality. Second, and more important, they learned that there were effective treatments available. Within days of the initial diagnosis, Will began taking medication and seeing a therapist. In a matter of weeks his behavior, though thankfully not his fundamental personality, began to change.

His grades, his relationship with friends, his athletic performance, even his dating prospects improved dramatically. By the time he graduated from St. Jude's, he had established a reputation as one of the brightest, most disciplined and likable kids in school. His success continued through college, during his three years in advertising, and through his two stints at graduate school. And during that time, Will never missed a daily dose of medication.

But, like so many people who rely on medication for mental health, Will decided it was time to take on his disorder by himself. A few months between school and work seemed like as good a time as any.

So, three weeks before his interview with Casey, Will decided not to renew his prescription. Within just a few more weeks he would begin to feel the full impact of having less of the chemical in his head.

FIREWORKS

Will's first day on the job was Thursday, July 2nd. He spent most of it meeting the few people who were working the day before a three-day weekend and learning how to check his new boss's e-mail and voice mail. While he was pretty sure it wouldn't be a difficult assignment, he hoped it would at least be interesting. As much as Will was looking forward to a little rest, he knew he had no tolerance for being bored.

By the time he arrived for his first real day of work on Monday, Will would stop worrying about being bored.

Going to his cubicle just outside his new boss's office, he looked in and found Casey sitting at his desk staring at his computer screen, almost catatonic. Will could see over his shoulder that Casey had been reading e-mail. Not knowing whether this apparent daze was normal, Will hesitated, and then knocked on the slightly open door.

"Good morning."

Nothing from Casey. Feeling extremely awkward, Will went back to his desk, turned on his computer, and while he waited for it to boot up, checked voice mail. Nothing urgent. He glanced at Casey's e-mail in-box. Fifty-three messages. He considered looking through them, but decided he needed to do something more important first.

Most new employees would have steered clear of the boss's office until he spoke to them, but Will was not like most people. He went back to see what was up. Casey was no longer staring at his computer; his head was bowed down now, almost touching the top of his desk.

Will walked in. "Are you okay, Casey?"

No response again. Even Will felt a little uncomfortable now. *This is one of my dad's favorite people in the world?*

And then, slowly, Casey raised up and turned toward Will, squinting at him just slightly as if he were assessing his worthiness. In reality, what he was doing was trying to decide what, if anything, to confide in his new assistant.

But then he realized, *Who else can I talk to?* Sure, he would try to discuss the situation with Patricia later that night. But ever since child number four arrived he had come to accept that there was only so much time and bandwidth she could dedicate to counseling him through work issues. As such, she had fallen slightly out of the loop when it came to the office. Right now he needed to talk to someone at work.

As much as he would have liked to, Casey couldn't confide in his staff members. Not about something like this. He had always prided himself, inappropriately so, on keeping big problems from them.

And he certainly would never have thought to talk to Gia about serious work issues. As much as she cared for her boss personally, she just didn't seem all that interested in the bigger picture.

So Casey tried to convince himself that Will was different. For one, he was the son of a very close family friend. And apparently a bright kid. Moreover, he wasn't really a Yip employee; he'd be gone in a few months anyway. Perhaps most important of all, he happened to be standing right there. *Why not?* Casey reasoned with himself in desperation.

"Shut the door, Will, and sit down."

Once Will had parked himself in front of the desk, Casey began. "I'd like to run something by you. I'd appreciate it if you'd keep it between the two of us. I wouldn't normally share this kind of information with Gia or anyone else."

Will nodded, accepting the responsibility.

"I told you during your interview that we might be under the microscope for a while. Well," he paused, "it looks like someone from Playsoft wants my job."

Will took it all in.

Casey was surprised, and relieved, to find that he wasn't embarrassed by the painful admission to a subordinate. He attributed it to Will's countenance, which seemed to be a delicate mix of empathy and confidence.

He continued. "Anyway, he's extremely political and he's going to make the summer a long one for me."

Will was confused. For a man who had built his company from scratch and had just been notified that it might be taken away, Casey seemed more resigned than angry. Something was missing.

"So who is this guy, anyway?"

"His name is J.T. He's the head of business development."

"Is he your boss?"

"Not exactly. Technically, I report to the CEO, but this guy's the CEO's right-hand man. And he put together the deal with us. He can probably make the call himself."

As the gravity of the situation hit him, Will understood why this reportedly extraordinary man was so down. So he did what came naturally—moved to problem-solving mode. "What are we going to do about this?"

Just then the phone rang. Casey ignored it. After considering the question for a moment, and letting the phone ring again, he finally replied, "I really don't know."

Will wanted to put his arm around his father's former pupil, who suddenly seemed helpless.

The phone rang for the third time and Casey glanced down at the caller identification screen. "Listen, I should probably take that. I'll see you at the staff meeting at ten. Thanks, Will."

Closing the door behind him, Will left the office feeling depressed.

But by the time he returned to his cubicle, he felt strangely and suddenly rejuvenated. *This job is going to be meaningful after all.*

It was at that moment that Will Petersen decided he would do whatever he could, no matter how small, to help one of his father's favorite people in the world save his job, and his company. And with forty-five minutes until the staff meeting, he figured he might as well start thinking about how he would go about doing that.

SMOKING GUN

Sitting down at his desk, Will decided to go through Casey's e-mail and then spend the rest of the day figuring out what was happening at this wacky company. Scanning the in-box, one name immediately jumped out at him—*J.T. Harrison.*

At first Will hesitated, feeling like he was violating Casey's privacy. Then he remembered that he was actually being paid to read his boss's e-mail, and clicked on the message:

> Casey,
>
> Tony said you wanted to talk to me. Sorry it's taken me so long. I've been traveling all week and too busy to call. So I thought I would send you this message and give you a little more information about why I'm going to be spending more time in Monterey this summer.
>
> As you know, we're under a little pressure right now as a company, given our anemic stock price and our revenue last quarter. And so everyone's coming under more scrutiny these days.

Anyway, I'll get right to the point. I'm having doubts about your ability to run your division. I'm basing that on a variety of factors, including intuition. But mostly, it has to do with my visit a few weeks ago. I have rarely seen such an unproductive, uninspired meeting in my career. I'm certainly hoping it was an aberration.

We can discuss this further during my visit in two weeks.

Until then,
J.T.

Will read the message again, amazed at how casually this guy had announced his possible intention to ruin Casey's world, and how ridiculous it seemed to base such an important declaration on the observation of one meeting. Not to mention that he had chosen to communicate it all via e-mail.

Suddenly Will was anxious for the staff meeting to start.

PART FOUR

Action

FIRST HALF

Staff meetings were held every Monday morning at ten in what was called the Upstairs Board Room, a large, modern conference room looking out toward Monterey Bay.

Will was determined not to be late, so he arrived five minutes early. Four and a half minutes later he started to panic when no one had shown up, thinking that he might have been in the wrong place. Just as he was about to leave, Casey entered the room, followed by Sophia and Connor, who were discussing sales and marketing. As soon as they saw Will, they stopped and greeted him warmly.

"How's the new guy doing?" Connor asked.

Will smiled.

Sophia joked, "You know, if you quit now you don't have to put this job on your résumé." They laughed, and made small but enjoyable talk about Will's studies, recently released movies, and what he wanted to do now that he had graduated.

More than a few minutes later Matt and Michelle walked in. Matt introduced himself to Will. "How's the new guy?"

Connor teased his colleague. "That's what I said! You couldn't come up with anything original? You're supposed to be our inventor."

"I like to leave the clever words to you marketing people."

They laughed louder than Will thought the joke deserved, but then again, this was the corporate world.

"Where's Tim?" Casey wanted to know.

"Oh, I saw him a few minutes ago," Matt explained. "He said he'd be about a half hour late, but to start without him. He's doing some budget stuff with the IT department."

Will looked to see how Casey would react to the news. Nothing. "Okay, let's get started."

Will wrote the time down on his pad: 10:12 A.M. He decided he would put it in the minutes he was going to be typing up and distributing after the meeting.

"Okay, here's my agenda. And as always, I assume that everyone received the minutes from last week."

Everyone nodded, but no one made eye contact with their boss. Will was sure this was a sign that no one had read them. He had seen the same behavior in college when the professor had asked his class what they thought of the chapters they were supposed to have reviewed.

Casey continued, looking down at the agenda he was holding in his hands. "We can skip the first item for now. When Tim gets here we'll talk about the budget. Let's start with item number two. We'll have Michelle tell us about management training and the summer picnic. Then we're going to get an update about new product development from Matt. And after that Sophia will take us through the sales pipeline."

Connor raised his hand and spoke. "I've brought the branding and advertising stuff I've been working on, and I'm prepared to go over it if anyone wants to see it."

After scanning the room and seeing mostly nodding heads, Casey agreed.

While they were waiting for Michelle to fire up her computer, Sophia made small talk. "Hey, we aren't doing the picnic at the high school again, are we? I think it was better when we just went down to the beach."

Matt responded. "I think we have too many people for the beach. But there's a new park in Carmel that would work."

"The one off of St. Mary's Road?"

Matt nodded. "My in-laws live down the street. It's nice, and big enough for us."

Her computer now operational, Michelle dove into the conversation. "I looked into that park, but it's taken already. The high school was our only option. Next year I'll reserve one of the Carmel parks early."

In spite of Michelle's proclamation, the conversation continued. Will listened in disbelief as the executives spent almost fifteen minutes discussing the merits of the high school versus the beach versus the park. They talked about the cleanliness of the bathrooms, the parking, and the need to make sure that the food was safe for a few of the kids who were allergic to peanuts.

Will took constant and copious notes just to overcome his sudden temptation to blurt out a rude comment.

Thankfully, Casey broke in. "Okay, that's enough about the picnic. Let's hear about management training."

For the next thirty minutes, Michelle reviewed her plans. Everything from the consulting firm she was planning to hire to conduct the training, the probable cost of the training, even the location where the training would most likely be held. Not once was she interrupted by her colleagues with an inquiry or a comment.

"Any questions?" she asked mercifully.

Nothing. Until Matt spoke. "Yeah. Do I have to go to this?"

Everyone laughed. Sophia threw a wadded-up piece of paper at her sarcastic colleague.

Casey wanted to move onto the next subject. "Seriously, though, are there any questions?"

Connor spoke next. "I'm just wondering if we need to do this. That $75,000 could buy me five solid trade publication ads. And given the company's stock performance lately. . . ."

"I know. I know," interrupted Casey with a smile. "All of us could use the money. But this is something we need to do, and we're not going to rob Peter to pay Paul."

Will was surprised that Connor put up no further fight.

Casey thanked Michelle for her time and effort, and Tim arrived.

Within minutes the CFO had launched into a detailed description of the company's budget for the next fiscal year. He went through each department—Sales, Marketing, Product Development, Finance, and Administration—in detail, as though he were doing one-on-one sessions with each executive while the others watched sleepily.

At one point the group spent ten minutes discussing whether the company should start shredding its own documents rather than bringing in an outside company, a move that could save the firm $72 per month.

Again, Will took notes to distract himself, all the while watching the clock slowly tick off the minutes and seconds. Finally, after almost forty-five minutes of financial discussion, Casey called for a ten-minute break. Which meant that the team would have just thirty minutes to cover new products, the sales pipeline, and possibly branding when they returned.

Will decided that he hadn't been this bored since his freshman year of calculus. *And to think these people are in the business of selling games that are actually fun to play. Maybe J.T. Harrison has a point after all.*

SECOND HALF

When everyone eventually trickled back into the room almost fifteen minutes later, Casey asked Matt to present the new product plan. He showed sketches of a variety of possible new games having to do with everything from long-driving contests and miniature golf to archery and equestrian. Everyone had questions about the features of the games and opinions about how they would be received in the market.

"Is anyone really going to buy an archery game?" asked Tim. "And isn't that a little violent?"

Matt was just slightly incredulous. "Archery? It's an Olympic sport. And they're not shooting cowboys or zebras. They're aiming at targets."

"Okay, but will people buy it?"

Conscious of the time, Casey interrupted. "We can have this conversation another time. Don't forget that Matt and Connor have been doing some market research. Let's move on to sales."

Sophia remained seated and quickly reviewed the numbers, breaking them down by week, month, and quarter-to-date. She announced a likely decrease in orders at golf course pro shops, and hoped that would be offset by an increase in toy store sales.

Casey was particularly interested in the trend at golf courses, and Sophia explained that pro shops seemed to be opting for more and more clothes instead of novelty items. And she mentioned that a few gaming competitors, most notably Gamestar, had made small but noticeable inroads into Yip's dominant position there.

For the next ten minutes the group speculated about why this had happened, and what they could do to avoid further damage. Was it the economy? Pricing issues? Market saturation? The weather? Will stopped taking notes now, for the first time finding himself genuinely interested in the conversation. But it ended as abruptly as it had started when Sophia, Connor, and Casey agreed to meet separately to explore how they might be able to regain shelf space in pro shops.

As the clock ticked down to less than five minutes remaining, Sophia read aloud the list of fifteen accounts she would be visiting or calling during the week. Everyone listened politely, but seemed to be mentally ready for the meeting to end.

Casey then turned to Connor. "I think it would be better if you went over the branding material next week. We aren't going to be able to give you the time you deserve."

Connor didn't seem even mildly disappointed. "Fine."

Casey proudly proclaimed the meeting to be over.

Tim joked, "And with a full minute to spare before noon."

As the room broke up, Casey asked, "Anyone want to come to lunch with me and Will?"

Tim and Sophia agreed. Connor and Matt apologized, explaining that they had other plans.

As the lunch foursome headed for the stairwell, Tim turned to Will and asked lightheartedly, “So, what did you think about your first staff meeting?”

Will froze. His notebook and pen were packed away, and as hard as he tried, he couldn’t hold in his answer: “It was really bad.”

Silence. Sophia shot a glance at Casey to see how he would react. Tim seemed to pretend that he hadn’t heard the comment, and entered the stairwell. The others followed, and for a long few seconds, no one spoke.

Will felt awful. The last thing he wanted to do was embarrass Casey in front of his staff. He stammered and tried to cover for himself. “I mean, it just seemed like. . . .”

Casey interrupted to defuse the awkward moment, for his own sake and for Will’s. “Yeah, I think it could have been better too. Sometimes I think we shouldn’t have meetings at all.”

They all chuckled politely. Sophia tried to soften the situation. “I’m just glad they don’t drag on like they used to.”

“You said it,” Tim agreed.

Will cursed himself as he followed his new colleagues out the main entrance and toward a restaurant across the street.

ON THE TABLE

Casey spent much of the afternoon, as he had so many others since the merger, on a conference call with other Playsoft division heads. Today they were going over sales projections. When he emerged, he seemed a slightly different man from earlier in the day. Less worried, more determined.

"Will, could you come in here for a moment?"

Feeling bad about his comment in the stairwell, Will decided to head off any reprimand that might be coming. "Casey, I'm sorry for being so blunt before—"

Casey interrupted. "That's what I want to talk to you about."

Will shrunk in his seat, waiting for the rebuke.

"I told you to dive in and help me in any way you could. So don't feel bad about what you said. You might want to hold your observations until you and I have a chance to talk privately, but don't worry about it."

Will couldn't decide whether or not Casey had been hurt by the remark. Whatever the case, he decided this was a good opening for him. "I should tell you that I saw the note from J.T." Will seemed to be confessing.

"Good. I'm expecting that you're looking through all of my messages. What did you think?"

"About his message? I thought he was a little blunt." The irony wasn't lost on either of them.

"Yeah, that's the reputation he has. He's looking for something to hang his hat on here. But he's not going to find it in our numbers. We're doing better than most of the company's other divisions."

"What about the meeting issue?" Will asked, reluctantly retreading on thin ice.

Casey smiled dismissively. "I think it's just a ridiculous excuse to get his foot in the door. Besides, our meetings aren't any worse than every other department in this company." It wasn't a question, but he was hoping for a response.

Will decided to throw Casey a bone. "Yeah, now that you mention it, staff meetings at the ad firm were horrible."

Casey was momentarily relieved.

Until Will continued. "But I'm not sure that matters."

"What do you mean?"

"I mean, if that's what he's focused on, then it's a real problem. Like you said, he can probably make the call himself."

Casey considered it. "Well, I think he's probably just fishing." He suddenly seemed to be retreating again. "Anyway, the most important thing is that we start to show an improvement on the bottom line." Casey looked at his watch. "I've got to run, but let's talk about this more tomorrow."

Casey left, and Will found himself feeling almost as bad as he did before. Not just because he had embarrassed a good man in front of his staff, but because that man wasn't taking a grave situation seriously.

WET FEET

True to his personality, Will immediately made a strong impression on the people he worked with.

In addition to quickly learning the administrative ropes and keeping Casey and his staff connected, he began to establish individual relationships with the team. It didn't take more than a few days for it to become clear to everyone that Will was not really an administrative assistant. And so they gave him more and more work to do, at an increasingly higher level. He easily exceeded their expectations, and as a result, established himself as more of a peer than a subordinate.

And in other parts of Yip's office, Will made a quick impression. Rather than return an e-mail to someone sitting a floor below, he would go see people in person and talk about what they really needed from Casey. As a result, he reduced the constant distractions that normally plagued his boss, and collected a hoard of new friends in the process.

Even outside of Monterey, Will made connections, most notably with the administrative assistants who worked for the company's other division heads around the country and in

San Jose. In a remarkably short time he had established a small network, if not a fan base, throughout the organization.

As much as this pleased him, Will couldn't stop wondering about Casey's dilemma with J.T. Harrison. He decided that the next staff meeting would somehow be different; he only hoped he would be able to restrain himself.

BAD SEQUEL

On Monday morning at ten o'clock sharp, Will again found himself sitting alone in the Upstairs Board Room. But eleven minutes later, the meeting was in full swing.

Casey passed out an agenda and started by announcing a new corporate edict calling for modest budget cuts. Tim followed with a half-hour review of where those cuts might come from.

Just as everyone was about to doze off, Sophia decided to put a question on the table. "Casey, I know you feel strongly about this, but do you think we might want to postpone the management training, and even scale back the picnic, in light of these numbers?"

As usual, Connor relentlessly reminded him, "And if we need to jump-start revenue, we could certainly use the money for advertising."

"It's too late." Tim announced, before his boss could weigh in. "We just prepaid on the picnic, and we're committed to the hotel and consultants for the training. If we canceled either now, we would only recoup about 25 percent of our cost."

The group accepted the CFO's assessment, and Casey was ready to move on. "Let's talk about how we can grow our revenue so the expenses aren't such an issue."

Sophia presented her sales forecast for the rest of the month and quarter, and recounted her previous week's visits with customers. She drifted off on a tangent about increased airline fares. Somehow, everyone found this interesting, and weighed in about their own experiences flying discount airlines.

Will scribbled notes to keep himself from screaming *stop!*

Finally, Connor stood to kick off his presentation about branding and positioning. For the next half hour he explained the need for the company to reposition itself against new competition, and to solidify its status as the dominant player in reality-based sports games focused on adults.

Will found this fascinating, harking back to his days in advertising. And given what was going on in the market, it seemed the right topic for everyone to be discussing.

Tim raised his hand and interrupted without waiting to be acknowledged. "Excuse me, Connor, but how much is all of this going to cost?"

Caught slightly off guard, Connor considered the question for a moment. "Well, I thought we were pretty clear about it. The consulting work and initial design phase has already been almost fifty thousand. And the brand launch will be another two hundred to two-hundred-fifty grand. That includes new business cards, signage, packaging. All told, we're talking about somewhere north of a quarter of a million."

"I've only seen about a hundred grand in your budget," questioned Tim. "Where is the rest going to come from?"

Casey jumped in. "Remember now, I arranged for another

hundred thousand from Playsoft when we put the deal together. They knew we were planning to rebrand and agreed to pitch in so we could do it right. So that only leaves us fifty thousand short. I thought we'd each kick in ten thousand to cover the additional cost."

Sophia wanted clarification. "Is that in addition to our picnic allocation?"

"Picnic allocation?" Matt was confused. "I didn't know there was a picnic allocation. I thought Tim was paying for the picnic this year."

It was at that moment that Will's pen ran out of ink. Panic. He looked around the room to see if he could find a spare one somewhere near the conference table, and he even considered taking one out of the hand of one of his colleagues. Finally, he gave up.

"Excuse me, but does anyone else think we should finish talking about rebranding this company before we waste another precious hour in pointless discussion about the damn picnic?"

The room went silent. For a long seven seconds.

Will wanted to retract his comment, but found himself digging a deeper hole. "I'm sorry, but these meetings are amazing. You guys spend more time getting less done and avoiding anything remotely interesting. . . . " He didn't finish the sentence, but just shook his head.

Everyone looked at one another as if to say *who's going to speak first?*

Finally, Casey took charge. "Why don't we take a ten-minute break. Let's be back at 11:15."

The room emptied, leaving just Casey and Will.

COMING CLEAN

When the doors had all closed, Will looked up and saw that Casey was smiling. "Wow. Where did that come from?"

Will decided to come clean. "Listen, there's something I didn't tell you about me. I've got this thing—"

"You mean the disorder?"

"Yeah, how did you know?"

"I'm a friend of your parents, remember. They told me about it when you were having trouble as a kid. But I thought you conquered it when you were in high school."

"I did. But I stopped taking my meds a few weeks ago, and I guess I'm having a hard time containing myself." Will took a deep breath, digesting his frustration. "I'll apologize to everyone when they come back. And I'm going to start taking my medication again. But it might be a few weeks before it kicks in."

"That's fine." Casey was being remarkably genuine and gracious. "You know, I knew a guy on the tour who had Tourette's Syndrome. He swore all the time, even when he made good shots. Great golfer." For the next few minutes they talked about Will's particular disorder. Casey showed remarkable concern, and Will could now say he understood why his dad liked this man so much.

As the break time was coming to an end, Casey assured his new assistant, "Don't worry, they'll understand."

THE SPARK

When the team returned, Matt raised his hand. Casey acknowledged him.

"I need to say something about Will's remark."

Will wanted to die.

Casey came to his rescue. "Listen, Will and I already talked about it and he feels bad that—"

Matt interrupted. "No, I'm not complaining about what he said. I think he's right. These meetings are still terrible."

Suddenly Casey felt uncomfortable, and decided to go on the defensive. "Come on now, we all know meetings are a pain. But do you really think ours are any worse than every other department in the company?"

Everyone seemed to be considering the question, some nodding in agreement with Casey.

But as usual, Tim pushed a little. "I don't know if they're worse or not. But whatever the case, we don't get much out of the two hours we spend every week sitting in this room. And aside from the time itself, I find it kind of draining."

The room seemed to collectively agree. Everyone was loosening up now.

Sophia went next, smiling. "You know, this reminds me of a job I had when I was in college. I was a bank teller during summer vacations, which I found to be extremely boring, given my personality."

Everyone chuckled at the thought.

"Anyway, I used to stare at the clock on the wall next to my station, just waiting for the next break, or for the day to end. I swear that sometimes the hands went backward."

They laughed again.

She continued. "Sometimes I look at that clock," she motioned to the one on the wall at the end of the table, "and I think I'm back at the bank."

In spite of the laughter in the room, Casey felt the sting of Sophia's comment.

Connor jumped in, directing his remarks at his boss. "Listen, it's not like we all don't hate meetings. I mean, I wish we could skip them altogether. This is not about you, Casey. It's just one of the necessary evils of business, I think."

Casey appreciated Connor's kindness, but wasn't about to let himself feel better. "Maybe. Anyway, let's get this one over with so we can get some real work done. We can deal with this later."

Connor resumed his discussion of branding for another five minutes. At precisely noon, he stopped and Casey called the meeting to a close.

Will walked away feeling terrible about bringing this on Casey, and more important, frustrated that he didn't know how to help him. He was determined to change that.

FALSE HOPE

When Sunday evening rolled around, Will found himself dreading the next morning's staff meeting for many reasons.

For one, those were the two slowest hours of his week. Now he knew why the other executives found any excuse possible to be late to meetings, or miss them altogether.

Beyond the boredom, however, Will feared blurting out another uncomfortable comment and wearing out his welcome with Casey. But more than either of these reasons, he just didn't want to watch his boss suffer.

So, to take his mind off work, Will went to his parents' house to watch a movie.

Now, Will wasn't the sort of film student who only liked movies subtitled in French. He enjoyed silly comedies and action movies as much as the next guy. But whenever he was home, he attempted to expand his parents' cultural horizons by trying to convince them to expose themselves to the kind of film that they wouldn't normally see. Fifty percent of the time he lost. Tonight he lost.

So he rented *When Harry Met Sally,* one of his parents' favorites. Invariably, two things would happen when he watched the movie with them: his dad would say, "Billy Crystal is not only funny, but he's a talented actor"; his mom would fast-forward through the infamous scene in the restaurant. Will loved being home.

After watching the film—for the sixth or seventh time in his life—Will scoured the DVD case, looking for the running time of the film. *Ninety-six minutes.* And suddenly it dawned on him.

A crew of thousands of men and women working with tens of millions of dollars required only one and a half hours to tell a story that spanned more than ten years in the lives of two people. The characters met, they didn't like each other, they hooked up with other people, they broke up, they became friends, they fell in love and they got married. All in ninety-six minutes! And with complete resolution.

Unbelievable. Will thought. *At work we take longer than that to summarize just a week's worth of business activity, and even then we never seem to resolve anything!*

Convinced that the big problem with weekly staff meetings was simply their length, Will suddenly was anxious for work to start the next day.

CHANGE-UP

He arrived early, eager to talk to Casey before the staff meeting. And then he turned on his computer and learned two pieces of information that would crush whatever momentum he had brought with him to work.

First, Casey's calendar indicated that he had a dentist appointment and would not be coming in until right before the staff meeting. Worse yet, J.T. Harrison had e-mailed to announce that he'd be attending that morning's meeting. Will reluctantly decided that he would have to wait to share his insights about shortening the meetings until the following week, and so he shifted his focus to damage control.

As luck would have it, J.T. arrived a little early. He approached Will's cubicle. "Where's Casey's assistant?"

"That's me. Gia's on maternity leave. I'm filling in for her for a while." He reached out his hand. "I'm Will."

"Nice to meet you, Will. I'm J.T. Harrison. Is Casey around?"

"He should be here any minute. He had a dentist appointment."

"Alright. I'll be up in the conference room for the meeting."

"See you there."

As soon as he was gone, Will felt a strange sense of disappointment. Though the man was certainly arrogant, Will had hoped that J.T. would be more detestable. He had pictured him as some sort of ruthless corporate titan, but in reality, he seemed nothing more than a slightly overconfident executive. Then Will thought back on the callous e-mail that J.T. had sent to Casey, and retrieved his temporarily diminished feelings of enmity.

Shortly after J.T. left, Casey arrived and went to his office. Will followed him in.

Before Will could say anything, Casey mumbled, in a barely discernible voice, "My mouth is numb. The darn dentist wasn't supposed to give me novocaine today. Before I knew what he was doing, he had me drooling."

Casey and Will shared a brief moment of laughter at the situation, especially the way Casey pronounced "dwooling." They sobered up quickly when Will informed him that J.T. was upstairs, waiting to observe the meeting.

Before Casey could utter any more mangled words, Will took charge. "Okay, I'll help you pull together the agenda. Did anyone send you any suggestions?"

Casey rolled his eyes and shook his head.

"Fine. Let's see. What should we talk about?"

Casey paused, then managed to spit out "budgets."

Will agreed and typed away. "But let's not lead with that. It's such a momentum killer."

Abandoning speech, Casey went to the white board. He wrote *sales, branding, competitive analysis,* and *IT.*

"What's the IT issue?" Will wanted to know.

Casey wrote *merging our systems with Playsoft's* on the board.

"Got it. Let's call it systems integration."

Casey shrugged as if to say, "Fine." He paused again, considering what else to add.

Will headed him off. "That's enough. Let's keep this meeting short and sweet. I don't want J.T. being bored again, and I'd love to get him back to San Jose by lunchtime."

Casey reached to his desk, grabbed two pens and handed them to Will. "Here. Take lots of notes," he commanded in slow and deliberate speech.

Will was distracted and didn't understand what Casey was after. "I will. But you know, I don't think anyone really reads the minutes."

Casey smiled and shook his head at his assistant. Suddenly Will realized that Casey didn't want him running out of ink and saying something inflammatory in front of J.T. Harrison.

Will laughed, and they left for the stairwell.

FAST BALL

In what amounted to herculean orchestration on the part of Will, for the first time in years the staff meeting actually started on time with the entire team sitting around the table.

Casey handed out copies of the agenda to everyone, including J.T., and dove right in. Speaking slowly under the influence of his local anesthetic, he explained, "I'm still not speaking too well this morning, as you can tell. So I'll let you all do most of the talking until I can feel my face. Will is going to be my proxy for a while." Again, his pronunciation of "pwoxy" brought everyone to laughter, including J.T.

Will began. "Let's start with a quick sales report from Sophia." It would be the first of many times that Will used the word *quick* during the meeting.

Sophia reviewed her numbers in detail, and then discussed her most recent visit with Target Stores in Minneapolis, going off on a tangent about the Mall of America. As the clock marked ten thirty, Will could see that J.T. was beginning to fidget, so he found a good moment to jump in and end the presentation.

"Okay, thanks, Sophia. Let's get a quick update on branding."

He looked to Connor, who began. "Okay, we're getting closer to having something to show you all. The design firm is in the process of mocking up logos and packaging that will reposition us as a younger, more exciting brand, while still differentiating us from our more juvenile competitors."

J.T. raised his hand, and as soon as Connor acknowledged him, he began. "Who are you positioning against?"

It seemed like an innocuous enough question, and Connor responded confidently. "Gamestar and GoBox, primarily."

J.T. pressed him. "What do you mean, primarily? Are there others?"

The room froze, eager for their colleague's response.

"Well," Connor considered the question, his confidence suddenly fading, "I guess they're the only two." Trying to regain some degree of momentum, he volleyed back. "Did you have someone else in mind?"

"Well, I'm just wondering if you shouldn't be thinking outside of the video game space. Do we need to be positioning ourselves relative to companies who are competing for the mindshare of our buyers?"

The room paused as if to consider the question, and to wait to see how Connor would respond.

He didn't have to because Casey jumped in, his diction already slightly improved. Still, he spoke a little slower than normal. "That's interesting. Maybe we should be looking at ESPN, or *Sports Illustrated,* or even on-line sports betting."

Everyone in the room, including J.T., seemed to find Casey's thinking interesting. They spent the next fifteen minutes throwing out ideas, and quickly established a list of possible candidates for comparison.

As the discussion abruptly died, Will was suddenly eager to introduce the next topic and set a new company record for the shortest meeting in Yip history.

But before he could, Matt dove in. As usual, the head of engineering spoke with more skepticism and accusation than he intended. "Who are these consultants you're using, anyway? Do they really understand our market?"

Connor looked like he had just been told he was a double agent working for the competition.

Will glanced at Casey, whose face said, "Uh-oh." Knowing that his boss wasn't in a great position to intervene, Will decided to take a chance.

"Okay, I don't think we need to be debating the merits of Connor's consultants right now. Why don't we pick this up again next week when we're looking at the logo mock-ups? We'll have more of a basis for evaluating them then."

Everyone nodded their agreement and the topic evaporated. Will decided it was a dexterous diplomatic move, averting a potential debate.

He continued. "Let's get a quick update from Matt on the systems integration with Playsoft."

The room seemed to wilt at the prospect of such an administrative discussion.

Matt proceeded to describe the time line and technical challenges associated with his IT department having to convert Yip to new systems for e-mail, voice mail, financial reporting, and asset tracking. Within fifteen minutes, the group had drifted into a coma.

Sensing the mood, Will moved things along again. "And Tim. Can you give us a brief summary of the budget process?"

"Sure, boss," Tim teased affectionately. Will blushed as everyone, including J.T. and Casey, laughed good-naturedly at their unlikely administrative assistant.

Tim then reviewed the budget shortfall and explained that the departments would be kicking in more than twice the previous year's allocation for corporate services. "That's because this year we have the picnic, the management training, and the branding shortfall."

Will could sense the frustration among his peers about having to pony up the additional money. But he knew that no one dared raise a stink, not with J.T. sitting among them.

It was now just eleven thirty, and Casey made the most bold and shocking announcement of the day. His novocaine seemed to have worn off considerably. "Okay, we've covered everything on the agenda, so if there's nothing else, let's go get some real work done."

Before anyone knew what was happening, a smattering of applause filled the room. The executives gathered their things and headed for the door without the normal sense of dull exhaustion that usually marked the end of the meetings. Will felt a sense of relief and satisfaction. It wouldn't last.

DETENTION

After everyone had left the room, Will gathered up his own things, erased the white board, and headed downstairs. As soon as he arrived at his cubicle, he sat down with a bird's-eye view of J.T. and Casey talking in Casey's office. Actually, J.T. was doing almost all the talking. Casey seemed to be biting his lip and enduring a mild scolding.

After almost half an hour, J.T. emerged and left the building without saying a word to anyone. Will hesitated for a moment, then went in to see Casey.

"How's it going?" he asked, somehow deciding that it was a little more subtle than *what happened?*

Casey shook his head. "Unbelievable. Absolutely unbelievable."

Will shut the door and waited for Casey to begin.

"First of all, he tells me that he was being *delicate* in his e-mail to me. He said he thinks our meetings are terrible, and that if they're any indication of how things are run around here. . . . " Casey stopped.

"What?" Will asked. "What did he say next?"

"Nothing. He just let it sit there."

Will wished he could have been in the room with them so he could have been delicate with J.T. "You should call Wade Justin and tell him to get this guy off your back."

"Well, it's funny that you mention him."

"Why? Did you call him?"

"No. But J.T. did. Right after our meeting."

Will's jaw dropped. "What?"

"He's coming out here with J.T. to observe a staff meeting in September."

The phone rang. Casey looked down to see who it was. "Speak of the devil."

"J.T.?"

Casey shook his head. "Wade Justin. Stay here."

Will didn't need to be convinced.

His boss picked up the phone. "This is Casey."

Amazingly, Will watched for three full minutes as Casey said virtually nothing, other than an occasional *yes, that's right,* or *I understand.* Finally, he ended the conversation unenthusiastically with "I appreciate it, Wade. Thanks."

As soon as he hung up the phone, Casey sat down at his computer to do some typing without acknowledging his assistant.

Will was incredulous. "Well?"

Casey looked up. "Oh, sorry. I was checking my calendar."

"So what did he say?"

Casey shook his head. "I don't understand this company. Wade Justin just told me that I shouldn't let J.T. intimidate me. He told me he has confidence in me, and that he knows I'm going to turn things around."

Will frowned. "Turn things around? What's that supposed to mean?"

"I don't know. But I do know that he'll decide whether or not it's happened when he comes to that meeting in September." Casey looked back at his computer. "Which is exactly five weeks from today."

"That is one bizarre company," proclaimed Will.

"No," countered Casey. "*This* is one bizarre company. We're part of it now." He paused for a moment. "At least for the next five weeks we are."

Will was suddenly wishing that his temporary job wasn't so interesting after all.

LIGHT BULB

The following week was the worst for Will since he'd arrived at Yip. More important, it was the worst for Casey since he'd founded the company.

For the first time in almost eleven years, Casey was forced to consider what he would do if he had to work somewhere other than Yip. He wasn't prepared, mentally or financially, to retire. And, like his employees, there was little else to do in the area without a master's degree in oceanography. *Am I going to have to leave this place?* he wondered.

Will sensed his boss's desperation and internalized it himself. On Sunday evening, he again found himself needing a distraction. And so he headed home to see his parents, but this time he wouldn't let his dad dissuade him from a "headier" movie.

Will chose an Italian film called *Cinema Paradiso,* subtitles and all. Not only that, it was the director's cut, meaning the filmmakers went back and added footage that had been edited from the first edition.

When the movie ended and Will's mom had wiped the tears from her eyes—Will even caught his dad welling up a little, but didn't want to embarrass him—everyone agreed that it was a terrific film. "I didn't even notice the subtitles after the first ten minutes, and that tells you something right there," his suddenly cultured dad announced.

Reaching for the DVD cover, Will wanted to know the length of the movie. He knew it was long, but was stunned by what he found.

One hundred and seventy minutes.

Will could not believe it. His father, the basketball coach, had sat still for almost three full hours watching a foreign film about a little boy, a man, and a movie theater.

Suddenly, Will began to think about some of his other favorite movies. *It's A Wonderful Life.* Well over two hours. *Braveheart.* Almost three. *The Great Escape.* Even longer.

And so it began to dawn on Will. The length of meetings had nothing to do with their effectiveness. Or did it?

Thoroughly intrigued, Will went home to Carmel and settled in for what would be his first all-nighter since college. Sitting down at his computer, he gathered around him a few textbooks from graduate school, most noteworthy of which were *Introduction to Film* and *The Screenwriter's Companion.* For the next five hours, Will was consumed with the challenge of finding a solution to his boss's problem.

By the time the sun rose, Will was amazed that, in spite of being so tired, he felt renewed. But it made sense. For one, he had finally convinced himself that he might be able to help Casey save his job. Additionally, he was actually excited about getting to the office so he could begin testing his theories in the real world.

PUSHING THE ENVELOPE

For the next two weeks, Will attended staff meetings—and any other meeting he could talk his way into—with the vigor of a zoologist studying the behavior of monkeys in the jungle. He observed Casey and his staff carefully, taking far more notes about his new hypothesis than about the minutes of the meetings themselves. *No one reads them anyway,* Will justified.

During the evenings, Will found himself reflecting on his observations from the day, and constantly refining his theory. Occasionally, he would discuss his ideas with his mother, who had just accepted a new job running a technology start-up just up the coast in Half Moon Bay. She found the theory interesting, and soon began applying it within her own company.

After pulling yet another Sunday all-nighter, Will decided that his theory was largely sound, and ready to be presented to Casey and his team. In spite of his sleep deprivation, he was energized as never before. Which was good, because he would need all the energy he could find in order to hijack Casey's staff meeting that morning.

NO PRISONERS

It had been almost a month now since Will had resumed taking his medication, and he was certainly feeling better. But it would be a few more weeks until he was back to normal, and lack of sleep only makes disorders like his more difficult to fight, no matter how much adrenaline, caffeine, or Prozac is rushing around one's system.

By the time the meeting started, Will was feeling a little funny but in control, or so he hoped.

Casey started the meeting by asking, "Where's Connor?"

"He has a meeting with one of his trade show vendors." Sophia explained. "He said he'd be here in an hour or so."

Casey seemed disappointed, but said nothing.

Suddenly Will felt the urge to make a comment about Casey's refusal to demand that his staff attend these meetings; the night without sleep had clearly taken its toll. To avoid saying something he would regret, Will pushed himself away from the table and stood, saying, "Excuse me. I'll be right back." And he left the room.

Walking down the hall, Will wondered what had just happened. *Why should I care if Casey lets Connor blow off his meetings?* And then it occurred to him that he needed everyone at the meeting if his plan had any chance of working. But rather than scold Casey publicly, Will bolted, heading directly for Connor's office.

As he approached, Will could see that the marketing VP's door was open. Connor was sitting behind his desk, working at his computer. Will knocked and came in without waiting for a response. "Excuse me."

Connor looked up calmly. "Hey, Will. What's up?"

"We have a meeting." Will said it as if he were asking a question.

"Yeah, I had to meet with one of the guys from TradeTech. I asked Sophia to tell Casey."

"So where is he?" Will pressed.

Connor was suddenly a little uncomfortable. "The guy from TradeTech? He left about five minutes ago. But I've got some follow-up work to do. I'll be in there by eleven o'clock."

Will just stood there, trying to determine whether it was his disorder or his determination that was forcing him to make the next statement. It didn't matter, because he couldn't hold back now. "You need to be there, Connor."

The head of marketing was puzzled, but not angry. Like his colleagues, he liked Will. "Excuse me?"

Will lightened up, but just a little. "Listen, this is an important meeting. For all of us, but especially Casey. Everyone needs to be there." He stared at Connor, almost pleading.

Connor studied Will for a second, considering the situation, and then responded matter-of-factly. "Okay then." He grabbed his notebook. "Let's go."

Relieved, Will accompanied Connor back to the conference room. When they entered, Casey looked at them, trying to discern what had happened out there.

Will decided that Casey had somehow figured it out.

The meeting continued as the newcomers sat down around the table. Tim was talking about budgeting, or something related to it.

Motivated by his successful intervention with Connor, Will decided not to wait. "Excuse me, everyone. I'm sorry to interrupt, but there is something that we have to do today. I'm afraid we'll have to postpone the items on the agenda until next week."

Tim and everyone else in the room were stunned. Except for Casey, who somehow seemed to be more curious than concerned about what Will was up to.

Before anyone could ask a question, Will began. "These meetings are not working, and they're causing more problems than we know."

Suddenly, Casey looked worried. He thought Will was about to explain the J.T. Harrison situation to the team, something that would be too uncomfortable for him to deal with right now.

Just as Casey was deciding to cut off his assistant, Will explained. "I've been talking to the people in this office for the past month or so, and you would be amazed about what they have to say."

That got everyone's attention.

"They're wondering about your, about our, competence. They just don't understand how we can come in here for two hours every week and emerge without clearer direction for them. Don't get me wrong. They seem to genuinely like you all. Which is why they're so confused by the output from these meetings."

As much as Casey wanted to end the meeting before it got out of hand, he was too intrigued not to hear what Will had to say.

Unsurprisingly, Tim spoke first. "Who did you talk to? I mean, are you sure that—"

Will interrupted him politely. "Listen, Tim. I'm not making this stuff up. Trust me."

Michelle supported Will. "What he's saying makes sense, if you consider what the survey indicated about decision making and communication."

"And besides," continued Will, "I've been watching it for more than a month, and I just don't understand how six smart and reasonable people can come in here week after week and continue to do something that, frankly, is a waste of time." Will paused as the team digested his remarks.

Before anyone—most likely Tim—could protest, Will completed his thought. "At least I didn't understand it until last night."

FILM SCHOOL

"What do you mean?" Casey was now hooked.

"I mean, I think I figured out why these meetings are less than productive." Will was trying to be polite. "And that's what we need to talk about today."

Sophia spoke next, and directed the question at Casey. "Can we afford to postpone the issues on the agenda for a week?"

The others in the room seemed to support her concern, and Will thought he was about to be overruled.

Then Casey reviewed the list in front of him. "Well, most of it could wait, I suppose. But we do need to talk about the Fall product launch and the budgeting deadlines."

Will jumped in, trying desperately to rescue his mission. "Okay, I'll tell you what. I'll give you thirty minutes to talk about those issues at the end of the session."

"A half hour?" Tim countered. "Come on."

Will resorted to pleading. "Just humor me. Please."

Because of the credibility that he had established with the team over the past few weeks, they agreed.

"Go ahead." Casey approved. "Give it a shot."

Will stood and went to the front of the room. "How many people here would rather go to a movie than a meeting?"

At first, no one raised their hands. They just sat there, looking at one another.

"Really. What is it? Movie or meeting? I want an answer."

Slowly, each person around the table said "movie," except for Tim, who said, "What are you, drunk? I'd rather go to the dentist than a meeting." Everyone laughed.

"Okay. What if I told you that meetings are inherently more interesting, more entertaining than movies?"

Unsurprisingly, Tim was first with the response. "Again, I'd say you were drinking too much." A little more laughter from the group.

Will pressed on. "Think about it this way. Movies and meetings are often approximately two hours in length, give or take twenty minutes or so. Right?"

A few nods from the group, so Will continued.

"But a movie is a passive activity. You can't interrupt one of the actors with advice about what to do. And yet a meeting is completely interactive. Not only can you, but you're expected to provide input."

The group was buying the point, but not connecting it to any larger issue. Not yet.

Will went on. "And a movie is not relevant to our lives. We don't have to go out and do something as a result of how a movie ends. Right?"

Will waited for a few more nods before continuing.

"But theoretically, meetings are completely relevant. The decisions that are made at the end of a meeting have a direct impact on how we spend our time and energy after we leave the room."

Now every head nodded.

"So I would say that an interactive, relevant activity—a meeting—would be far more compelling than a passive, irrelevant one—a movie."

The looks on everyone's faces seemed to concede that Will had made an interesting point.

Will took a breath. He was gaining confidence now. "So why do you suppose we would rather go to a movie than a meeting?" He paused, then continued. "That's not a rhetorical question."

Matt responded first. The tone of his voice suggesting that the answer was obvious. "Because meetings are boring and movies aren't."

Will nodded. "And why is that?"

No one seemed ready with an answer, so Will provided it for them. "Because screenwriters figured out long ago that there is one element required to make any movie interesting. And it's something we need in these meetings." He paused for just a moment before revealing that element. "Conflict."

The group still seemed a little confused, but there was no doubt in Will's mind that they were now hooked. "You see, a few weeks ago I was convinced that the problem with these meetings, and with meetings in general, was that they were too long. But then I realized that even really long movies can be amazing, as long as there is a compelling enough conflict to hold your interest."

"Wait a second," countered Sophia. "Not all movies have conflict."

Will accepted her challenge. "The good ones do. Give me a movie that doesn't have conflict at its very core."

Sophia didn't have an immediate answer, so Will took another tack. "Okay, everyone write down the name of your favorite movie."

The executives seemed to hesitate, as if they were wondering, "are you serious?"

"Go ahead. Write it down."

Like a kind old judge questioning a young attorney during a trial, Casey prodded Will, "I hope you're going somewhere with this."

"I am," he assured him.

Casey nodded, and everyone put pen to paper. After a minute or so, Will called for their answers, one by one.

Connor:	*Butch Cassidy and the Sundance Kid*
Sophia:	*The Sound of Music*
Matt:	*The Godfather*
Michelle:	*Top Gun*
Casey:	*Amadeus*
Tim:	*Hoosiers*

"Okay. Does anyone have any doubt that these movies are loaded with conflict?"

"What exactly do you mean by conflict?" Matt wanted to know.

Will launched into a sermon, of sorts. "Well, I'm not necessarily talking about war, or a fistfight, or even a shouting match, if that's what you're after. Conflict is nothing more than an anxious situation that needs to be resolved. Some conflicts are between two people, like *Rocky*. Others are about a person vying against nature, like *Jaws* or *The Perfect Storm*. And many of the best movies are about a person's internal conflict. In fact, most movies, even the action movies, are ultimately about a person's internal struggle. But no matter what is going on, there has to be something ultimately at stake. A prize, survival, sanity, success, even peace of mind."

After a brief pause, Tim spoke up. "So where's the conflict in *The Sound of Music?*"

Before Will could respond, Sophia was all over the CFO. "Are you joking? First there's Christopher Plummer's character, the captain, defying the Nazis. Then there's Maria competing with the baroness for the captain's affection." She continued sarcastically. "And you might not want to forget about the actual escape from Austria."

Michelle chimed in. "She even had conflict with the children at first, before they accepted her."

Will agreed and added. "And the most important conflict of all may have been the internal one, with Maria trying to figure out what to do with her life."

"Okay, okay, I believe you." And then Tim confessed. "You know, I've never actually seen the movie. I don't really like musicals."

Sophia was stunned, and teased her friend mercilessly. "You've never seen *The Sound of Music?* You really are a cretin, aren't you?"

They all laughed.

Tim decided to come clean. "I haven't even seen *The Godfather*."

Now the entire room was up in arms.

Tim defended himself. "The whole mob thing just doesn't interest me."

"But it's not just a mob story." Casey explained. "There are more mafia movies out there than you can shake a stick at, but *The Godfather* was much bigger than that."

Will was loving this, and played the role of professor. "So what was the conflict in *The Godfather?* Why is it so hard to stop watching once you start?"

Casey answered immediately and enthusiastically. "It's Michael Corleone trying to stay out of the mob, and then getting sucked into the family business until he is so deep he can't escape. It's fascinating watching this clean-cut kid with all the right intentions fight the temptation to go over to the dark side."

The others in the room were nodding and reliving the movie in their minds.

Will smiled. "And that, ladies and gentlemen, is why we like movies. Not the special effects. Not the big name actors. Not the popcorn. Not even the violence. It's the conflict. The human drama. That's what keeps us on the edge of our seats."

Matt raised his hand and actually waited for Will to recognize him. It was as if Will had suddenly become a professor, and his students were hungry for more.

"So, I agree that all our favorite movies have conflict. What I don't get is why our meetings need to have it too. I mean, sure, they won't be as boring. But how much of a difference is that really going to make in the long run?"

Will considered the question, wanting to find the right words.

Casey didn't let him. "Come on now, Matt. If we're engaged, don't you think we're going to be making better decisions? And we'll probably be more likely to get everyone's ideas and opinions out on the table."

"And that's one of the big problems with your meetings now," added Will. "Every time you guys are on the verge of getting into a crucial conversation about something that might get heated, you seem to bail out."

Matt nodded, but had another challenge for Will.

"Okay. But how are we supposed to compete with the Nazis and the mafia when it comes to drama? I mean, aren't we at a disadvantage? The stakes here are a little lower."

Will shook his head emphatically. "No. They're much higher."

People looked at Will as if he had just pronounced the world flat. But he had them right where he wanted them.

"The stuff you're supposed to be talking about here is more important for you than whether the Van Trapp family escapes from Austria is for moviegoers. Heck, the issues you talk about here are what puts bread on your tables and keeps you all employed. How much more could be at stake?"

No one argued.

Connor was suddenly eager to speak, so Will called on him.

"What about *Tommy Boy?* Where's the conflict in that?"

Michelle jumped in, joking. "He said the movies have to be good."

Everyone laughed, until Will defended Connor.

"*Tommy Boy* is one of my favorite comedies. Chris Farley was hilarious."

Connor felt redeemed. "So what was the conflict?"

Will smiled, and then dissected the movie as though it had won the Academy Award for best foreign film. "Well, to start with, Chris Farley is trying to save the company his father had built and run until he suddenly died. He has to fight off the subversive threats of Bo Derek and Rob Lowe."

Everyone, including Will, laughed at the pseudo-sophisticated analysis of a screwball comedy.

Undeterred, Will continued the lecture. "And most important of all, he has to confront his own maturity and self-worth in order to become the leader of the firm."

Connor smiled, both impressed and amused by the analysis.

Out of nowhere, Casey jumped in. He was suddenly a little impatient, even edgy. "Okay, so I suppose I'm the one who needs to make all this happen."

Will nodded, and Casey continued. "Given that I'm not naturally comfortable with conflict, how am I supposed to make sure our meetings have it?"

"The question isn't *how,*" Will explained. "It's *when.*"

THE HOOK

In full professor mode now, Will asked the question: "What is the most important part of a movie?"

No one responded, so Will persisted. "Come on now, if a movie is roughly two hours long, what is the most critical part of those two hours?"

Connor played first. "The end."

Will decided to have some fun. "How many people think it's the end?"

Most of the hands in the room went up. Will made a sound like a game show buzzer announcing the wrong answer. "ERRRR. Sorry."

Everyone laughed.

Tim shouted, "The turning point!"

Will waited for the room to quiet down, and then gave Tim the "ERRR! Wrong again."

More laughter.

Amid the noise, Casey spoke up. "The beginning."

Will pointed at Casey. "We have a winner. The beginning."

Everyone groaned playfully at having been outguessed by their boss.

Will continued. "And it's not just the beginning; it's the first ten minutes. Or the first ten pages if you're writing a screenplay." He paused to let them digest it. "Why do you suppose the beginning is so important?"

"First impressions," answered Matt.

"Right. If you lose people in the first ten minutes of a movie, if you don't hook them, you're through. They'll spend the rest of the movie, no matter how exciting it becomes, thinking, 'This is a good scene. Too bad it's such a slow movie.' But if you hook them at the beginning, they'll forgive a slow scene here or there."

Everyone in the room was nodding and smiling as if they were remembering a movie that supported Will's thesis.

Will knew they liked talking about movies, so he stayed on the topic. "Think about your favorite movies. You can probably remember the opening scenes. Something about them got your attention and hooked you. And that's what you have to do in your meetings. Give people a reason to care."

Casey had been taking notes, and suddenly looked up. "I don't see how you can make the beginning of a meeting as exciting as the opening scene of *Raiders of the Lost Ark*."

"I agree. It probably won't be as exciting." Will acknowledged. "But then again, people go to the movies expecting to be entertained. The bar is pretty high. For meetings, however, it shouldn't take much to get people's attention. People are generally accustomed to being bored out of their minds."

Everyone laughed.

"Can you give us an example of how you'd make a fairly dry topic compelling?" Casey was intent on figuring this out.

Will took a breath. "Sure. I hope I can. Let's see. Someone give me a topic that doesn't sound too interesting."

He waited. Finally Sophia said, "Budgets."

"Well, that certainly doesn't sound interesting," Will joked, to the amusement of his colleagues, including Tim.

He continued the lecture. "Okay. The subject is budget cuts. Tell me how we would normally start a budget review meeting."

Connor jumped in and took the opportunity to tease his CFO. "Tim would normally tell us to turn to page forty-two in our budget booklets, and then he would make each of us read aloud the line items in our spreadsheets where our budget amounts were more than 15 percent higher than last year's." Connor then feigned a yawn and fell face first on the table in front of him as though he had passed out from boredom.

The room howled.

Tim protested playfully. "Come on, it's not that bad." He let them keep laughing at him, and then looked at Will. "Actually, it's probably not far off."

Will tried to refocus the team. "Okay, how could you turn this situation around? What would your opening scene look like?"

No one had a clue.

"Alright. I'm going to give this a shot." Will smiled as though he were about to take a risk. "The role of Tim will be played by his understudy, Will Petersen."

They all laughed, and suddenly Will was in character.

He began, "I know that the next couple of hours might be tedious, and that there are a hundred other things we'd all rather be doing right now. But let's keep a few things in mind while we're here today. First, our competitors are hoping we get this wrong. They're hoping we underallocate resources for advertising, or hire too many administrative staff. And our employees are desperate for us to get this right, because every decision we make today has a profound impact on someone's job, not to mention their morale. In their minds, our credibility is on the line. And finally, I don't want to be sitting at my desk nine months from now thinking, 'Why didn't I pay closer attention during that budget review?' So let's sit forward in our seats and do this right so we can feel good about it for the rest of the year."

He paused, and after a few moments, the room broke out in mock applause.

Will blushed. "Okay, so that's not an academy award-winning performance, but it's a hell of a lot better than 'Please turn to page forty-two in your budget booklets. . . . "

Everyone laughed and nodded in agreement.

Casey then asked a question. "Okay, after those first ten minutes, then what?"

Though he was enjoying the discussion, Casey was certainly not as upbeat as everyone else in the room. The levity subsided a little when the others recognized this. Only Will knew that Casey was probably thinking about J.T. Harrison.

MINING

Will forged on. "It gets easier, I think, because the beginning is the hardest part. Once you've teed up the topic, then you just need to keep searching for conflict. When I was studying psychiatry, we used to call it *mining.*"

Casey was confused. "Mining?"

Will explained. "Everyone, but especially you, as the leader of the group, needs to be looking for places where people have different opinions but aren't necessarily putting them out there. And when you see that, you need to force them to communicate what they're thinking until they've said all there is to be said. You need to be constantly mining for buried conflict."

"Isn't that going to take a long time?" Matt wondered.

Will was surprised when Sophia responded. "What's the alternative? Not resolving it and having people come back in six months and say, 'Well, I never really agreed with that decision when we talked about it before?'"

Will could see that Casey was either unclear or uncomfortable about something. "What's up, boss?"

"Nothing," Casey said reflexively. "It's just that it sounds like people always have to come to agreement on things. And no matter how much time you take, I don't think that's always possible."

Will somehow seemed alarmed by Casey's comment. "Did it sound like I was advocating consensus?" A few heads nodded. "I'm glad you asked the question, Casey, because I didn't mean that at all! In fact, I think that consensus is a horrible thing."

Now Michelle looked confused. "How can consensus be horrible?"

Will qualified his comment. "Well, maybe I overstated it a little. But the point is, consensus is usually not achievable. The likelihood of six intelligent people coming to a sincere and complete agreement on a complex and important topic is very low."

"So what do you do?" Michelle wondered.

"You have a passionate, unfiltered, messy, provocative discussion that ends when the leader of the team decides all the information has been aired. At that point, if no one has made a compelling enough argument for making a decision, the leader breaks the tie."

The executives looked at each other as if to say, *Sounds good to me*.

Will punctuated his lecture. "But let me be very clear about something. Regardless of what position people originally took, once the decision is made, everyone supports it. That's why it is critical that no one hold anything back during the discussion."

Everything began to click for Casey. "And that's why we need to mine for conflict, regardless of what the clock says."

"Exactly." Will felt like he was making progress.

Matt decided to play devil's advocate, something he was particularly adept at. He challenged Will, in a slightly playful but mostly serious tone. "I'm sorry, but I think this is a bunch of touchy-feely nonsense. I don't think we need conflict. And I don't particularly like it."

Will remained calm. "Why do you suppose?"

Sophia didn't hesitate. "Because things get emotional and someone gets upset and the next thing you know everyone in the office is whispering about the executive team not getting along."

Will pushed back. "But they're already talking about the fact that you guys don't make decisions in these meetings."

Casey nodded, ceding the point to Will.

Now Matt challenged him. "See, I don't care about the emotional stuff. If people get upset or start talking about the executive team, I could care less. It's the waste of time that gets to me. I don't want to sit around and watch people debate all day. I'd prefer if Casey just made the call and we could get back to work."

"Are you kidding?" It was Sophia again, and she didn't wait for an answer to her completely rhetorical question. "I don't see how it could be any worse than it is now."

Matt seemed a little put off by Sophia's challenge. The room was tense for a moment, until Michelle jumped in.

"I have to agree with Sophia. We're already wasting so much time as it is, and we still don't seem to get to the bottom of things. Even if it did take up more time, at least it would be interesting. I'd rather spend three hours on something and come to the right decision than spend one hour and get nowhere."

Matt wasn't ready to give in just yet. "I'm not sure it would be interesting."

Casey countered. "What is the most interesting meeting we've had in the past six months?" He directed the question at Matt, who shrugged his shoulders.

Casey smiled. "Come on, it's obvious. It's this one, today. Look at us. We're actually involved in the conversation. People are disagreeing. It's interesting."

Matt nodded to acknowledge the point, while everyone just sat there drinking in the lesson.

Until Tim broke in. "Now wait a second. I thought that other meeting was pretty interesting, when Will told us to stop talking about the damn picnic."

They laughed.

"But there it is again," Casey reminded them, smiling. "Conflict."

PRACTICE

As much as Will wanted to stop right there and savor the victory, he knew that it was time to push forward. "Okay, you guys wanted to talk about real issues. Here's your chance. Let's take an issue and see if we can't mine it for conflict."

Casey was game. He directed a question at the group. "What should we start with?"

Michelle made the first suggestion. "The picnic."

Everyone roared. Except Michelle. "I'm serious. I think it's time we dealt with this issue once and for all."

Casey forced himself to play his role. "Okay, what's the real issue here?"

Michelle was a little upset. "I don't like being in charge of the darn picnic—"

Tim interrupted. "You mean, damn picnic."

Everyone, including Michelle, laughed momentarily. "Okay, damn picnic. I don't like being in charge of it any more than you guys would. I'm not an event organizer or a party planner, but since this is part of my job, I'm doing it. The thing is, I'm tired of hearing people complain about it, and about having to pay for it from your budgets. I mean, it's all coming out of the company's money anyway."

For just a moment, Michelle looked like she might actually cry. The room was silent, unaccustomed to raw emotion during meetings.

Casey wanted to let the issue drift away, but looked over at Will and decided to push a little. "Does anyone disagree with Michelle?"

No one spoke. Casey looked at Matt. "How about you? You're probably the most outspoken critic of the picnic."

The entire room seemed stunned by Casey's directness.

Michelle took the opportunity to pile on. "You might as well throw management training in there too," she said.

Now Matt was engaged. "Wait a minute. I said I'd go to management training, and I never complained about having to pay for that."

Michelle was taken aback by Matt's tone, and didn't look like she was going to respond.

Will waited to see if his boss would keep pushing, and when it didn't look like Casey would, he jumped in himself. "What do you think, Michelle?"

She took a deep breath. "I think it's not just about the money. It's about being supportive. If we don't think we need to train our managers, then fine. Let's decide that and I'll focus on something else." She was flustered now. "I don't know."

Everyone in the room was uncomfortable now.

Will spoke. "Okay, there are three important points I have to make here. First of all, this is the right conversation to be having. So you two," he motioned at Matt and Michelle, "should not be feeling like you're out of line."

He let the point sink in as Matt and Michelle seemed to take a small measure of consolation from the reminder.

"Second, that discussion was definitely not boring."

Everyone laughed, welcoming the humorous distraction.

"And third, we need to hear from everyone else." Will scanned the room to emphasize his point.

The laughter disappeared. After a pause, Tim spoke. "Well, I understand where Matt is coming from. I mean, I can't say I'm looking forward to management training—or the picnic either, for that matter." He looked at the head of HR. "But Michelle is right. We were all here when we agreed to do these things. And now that the commitment's been made, we should stop talking about it and make the most of it."

Sophia went next. "I'm good with that. But I do want us to get very clear about what is going to be different next time. It seems like we complain about these same things every year."

Somehow everyone was looking at Connor, who had yet to speak. When he finally realized that they were waiting on him, he said, "Don't look at me. I like the picnic."

They laughed again.

Matt finally spoke. "Look, when I complain about these things, I'm not directing them at you." He was looking at Michelle.

"But it certainly feels that way," she explained.

"I know. I think I'm just frustrated that we have so much to do, and we're wasting time on things that don't matter."

"Don't matter?" Sophia protested.

Matt backpedaled. "That's not what I meant. I know those things are important for employees. It's just that I think we need to be more focused on topics that involve making money. That's all."

Eager for closure, Casey brought the discussion home. "And so we're not going to waste any more time talking about management training or picnics. And next year, we'll sit down and put it all on the table during our planning, and make a decision and stick to it."

He then turned to Michelle. "You okay with all of this?"

She nodded. "Yeah. I'm just glad you all know that I'm only trying to do my job. And believe it or not, I would prefer that we spend more time talking about issues involving revenue too."

At that precise moment, Michelle's standing with Matt, and the rest of the team, increased dramatically.

The discussion then shifted to other topics: branding, sales strategy, information systems.

Each time, Casey tried to draw people out and highlight any differences of opinion. But he wasn't perfect. At times there were awkward lulls in the conversation, and confusion about what topics merited more or less attention. Still, it was a better staff meeting than any others they could remember.

But as the meeting ended, Will couldn't deny that his theory had fallen short of his high expectations.

Something's still missing, he thought to himself.

DRAWING BOARD

As disappointed as he was, Will decided that his theory about conflict was not completely flawed. It was just incomplete.

So he went back to his textbooks in search of more answers. *What else, besides conflict, is necessary to make a movie great?* he wondered. For the next week he read screenplays, watched movies, and examined notes from some of his classes, and found nothing.

He made more than one trip home to pick his mother's brain. Finally, the seeds of a solution began to grow.

One night as he was cleaning his room, he noticed his *History of Television* textbook on the floor of his closet. Some kind of spark ignited, and before he knew what was happening, Will found himself still reading at dawn.

By the time he had showered and was heading into work, it all began to make sense.

And so, Will went on yet another meeting binge. No matter how long or short, and regardless of the topic under discussion, he forced himself to sit through any meeting that he would be allowed to observe.

At night, Will watched television, changing channels constantly and reflecting on his evolving theory. And he called home for more motherly insights about business, which he would later look back on as being vital to his theory. By the time Sunday evening came around, he was exhausted. But hopeful.

With just two weeks now until the meeting, Will believed he actually stood a decent chance of helping Casey and his team crack the code on their big problem. What he didn't know was that he might not get a chance.

BOXED OUT

Will arrived at work on Monday eager to present his findings to the team. Before the meeting started, however, Casey called him into his office with an announcement he thought Will would like. He was wrong.

Casey explained that Playsoft needed volunteers to go to Chicago to help set up and manage the company's massive trade show booth at the annual Toy and Game Convention there. Before Will could tell his boss that he wasn't interested in volunteering, Casey informed him that he'd already been volunteered.

It was a ten-day gig at one of Chicago's nicer hotels. Moreover, Will could fly home for the weekend, or fly a friend to Chicago, or just stay there and pocket the airfare. Being a recently graduated student, Will would normally have jumped at the opportunity for extra cash or a free trip. But not this time.

"Listen, Casey, I need to be here. That meeting's coming up in two weeks, and we've got work to do if—"

Casey interrupted, politely. "I know. I know. But you really helped us a few weeks ago, so I think we'll be fine."

Will knew that Casey was less than convinced of this.

"And you'll be back a couple days before the meeting anyway."

Will pushed harder. "But it's not about me being there. It's about us figuring out how to—"

Interrupting again, Casey seemed a little annoyed now. "Listen. If J.T. Harrison wants to fire me, he's going to fire me. And if the only thing he can come up with is that our meetings are not as exciting as the circus, then there's nothing I can do about it."

Will wanted to scream *yes there is!* But he realized that Casey was already preparing himself for the worst, just in case. And if J.T. had indeed already made up his mind, then making Casey worry about the situation would be cruel.

Will couldn't believe the words were coming out of his mouth. "When do I leave?" He was clearly deflated.

Casey laughed. "Come on, Will. You're not going to war. You're going to Chicago. And they need you there tomorrow afternoon."

"So I could fly out on the red-eye tonight?"

"Sure. If you want to."

"Good. Then I'll see you at the meeting in a few minutes. And I'm going to need a little more time to talk about meetings if I'm not going to be around for the next two weeks."

Casey reluctantly nodded his approval.

Will left, knowing that the next two hours could be crucial for Casey and his company. He also found himself wondering if he should have applied for a job at Starbucks.

SECOND SEMESTER

As soon as everyone had settled into their seats for the staff meeting, Will stood to make an announcement.

"I'm sorry to do this again, everyone. But I need at least an hour today to talk about my meeting thing again."

Matt winced. Others looked around the room for kindred souls, but no one wanted to be the first to protest.

Casey stepped in to disrupt the awkwardness. "Listen, everyone, I think after last week we can give Will some time again. We'll have plenty of time to cover the items on the agenda."

Will was momentarily relieved.

Until Casey explained, "But you can only have a half hour. Starting now."

Now Will was worried. Not wanting to waste even a minute, he dove in. "Okay, you remember everything I said last week about conflict? It's wrong."

The people sitting at the table looked at him in disbelief.

Tim didn't hesitate. "You mean to say that—"

Will interrupted. "Relax. I was kidding."

They groaned, and laughed a little.

"But I have to admit that there is more to my theory than conflict. And unfortunately, it isn't as interesting."

The room seemed to take a collective breath, and steel themselves for boredom as Will went to the board and wrote *drama*.

Will continued, undeterred. "The biggest problem with our meetings, and with meetings in general," he paused for effect, "is structure." He wrote it next to *drama* on the board.

Sensing that he might lose his crowd, Will pushed forward in a more contrarian tone. "Our problem is not that we're having too many meetings. Our problem is that we're having too few of them."

Though he had regained their interest, the looks on the faces around the table seemed to suggest that he had lost all the credibility he had gained over the course of the past two months. What they didn't know was that Will had them right where he wanted them.

Will's White Board—The Missing Elements of Meetings

Drama	Structure

MULTIMEDIA

"I'm not saying we need to be spending more time in meetings, necessarily. But we definitely need to be having more than one type of meeting."

He brought the discussion back to media and entertainment. "Think about it this way. What if there were only one kind of television program?"

He went to the white board and picked up a pen, giving himself a few moments to collect his thoughts. Turning back to his audience, he asked, "Not everything we watch is a movie. What is the shortest program on television?"

Tim, like a third grader wanting to get the right answer first, responded, "A sitcom."

"Okay, a sitcom." Will did not write the word on the board. "But isn't there anything shorter?"

"Shorter than a half hour?" Sophia wondered out loud.

"Yeah. Is there anything on TV that you watch for less than a half hour?"

Something seemed to suddenly occur to Michelle. "*CNN Headline News.*"

"Right," Will responded enthusiastically, surprised and relieved that someone had figured out the difficult question. He wrote her answer on the board. "And how long do you usually watch *Headline News*?"

"Five minutes. Sometimes less." Matt offered.

"And how *often* do you watch it?"

Matt shrugged. "Every day. Why not?"

Will wrote the words *five minutes* and *daily* on the board next to *headline news*. "Okay, so in our first category of programs, if you will, we have *Headline News,* which is five minutes or so every day."

Still deep in the woods with his crowd, Will pushed forward.

"And in our next category we have sitcoms," he wrote the word on the white board, directly under the previous ones, and then wrote *crime drama* alongside it. "I'm going to combine sitcoms and one-hour shows about crime and hospitals and things like that. So we'll say that these are roughly an hour. And how often do we watch a given sitcom or docu-drama?"

He didn't wait for an answer to the obvious question, but wrote down *weekly* on the board next to *one hour.*

Will was sure that no one knew exactly where he was going. But he was also sure he had regained their attention, and for now, that's what mattered most.

"Next comes movies. Approximately two hours in length. Let's say we watch a TV movie, or for that matter, go to the movies, about once a month."

Connor teased Will. "You don't have kids, do you?"

All the parents in the room laughed.

After writing *movie* and *two hours* on the board below the others, he finished. "And last of all is—"

He paused to see if anyone could guess. When it was clear that they wouldn't he wrote the word *mini-series* at the bottom of the list, along with *six hours or more.*

"Now I know all this sounds crazy, but bear with me. Imagine if a network came out with an idea for a new two-hour weekly show that was designed to please all audiences. It was part mini-series, part movie, part sitcom and crime drama, and part headline news. Which of the different audiences would like that show?"

Michelle went first. "None of them would."

"Why?" Will asked.

"Well, because it wouldn't make any sense. It would be way too long for a sitcom, not long enough for a mini-series, and I don't even know how you could fit the *Headline News* in there."

"What about the part that is feature-length film?" Will liked the Socratic method.

Now Connor responded. "With everything else going on, it would be one terrible movie."

Will put down his pen deliberately and turned toward the slightly confused team. "So why then are we doing this very same thing when it comes to our weekly meetings?"

A few of the intellectual lightbulbs in the room seemed to be flickering now. Others were still dark. Will wanted complete understanding, so he pressed on. "We are trying to accomplish too many things during these painful Monday morning meetings, and we're not doing any of them successfully."

The team digested Will's assessment.

Will's White Board—The Missing Elements of Meetings

Drama	Structure
	Daily Headline News (5 min)
	Weekly Sitcom/Crime Drama (1 hr)
	Movie (2 hrs)
	Mini-series (6 hrs or more)

"But what does that have to do with a sitcom?" Tim wanted to know.

"Think about it this way. We should be having four different kinds of programs, each tailored for a given audience."

"I'm still not following you, kid." Tim sounded critical, but Will knew him well enough to know that it was just his style. "Isn't there only one audience? I mean, the same person watches *Headline News,* sitcoms, movies, and mini-series, right?"

Out of nowhere, Casey jumped in. "I think what Will's getting at is context."

Will turned toward his boss with a look of revelation on his face. "I hadn't thought of it that way, but that's probably right. Context." He considered the comment, suddenly energized by Casey's simple but important insight.

Casey explained. "A guy sitting down for a sitcom has very different expectations than he does when he's going to a movie. Or watching *Headline News* at the airport."

The leader of the company turned to Will. "Go on with your lecture."

THE DAILY CHECK-IN

Glad to have his endorsement, Will continued. "I'll get right to the point. I think we need to start having a *Headline News* every day, for five minutes. We could call it a Daily Check-in or something. That means we should get together in a conference room, standing up, and just announce what we're all doing."

"Every day?" Matt challenged.

"Every day." Will assured him. "Five minutes every day would save us countless e-mails and voice mails and office drop-ins. I know because I'm the one at the center of them all. 'Is Casey in the office today?' 'Who's coming to the marketing review this afternoon?' 'Does Casey want me to follow up with the lawyers, or should Tim do it?'"

Will's characterization made everyone smile in an embarrassed kind of way.

He continued. "Do you guys know how much time it takes just to clarify your daily expectations of one another?"

They seemed to be getting it now.

Will's White Board—The Missing Elements of Meetings

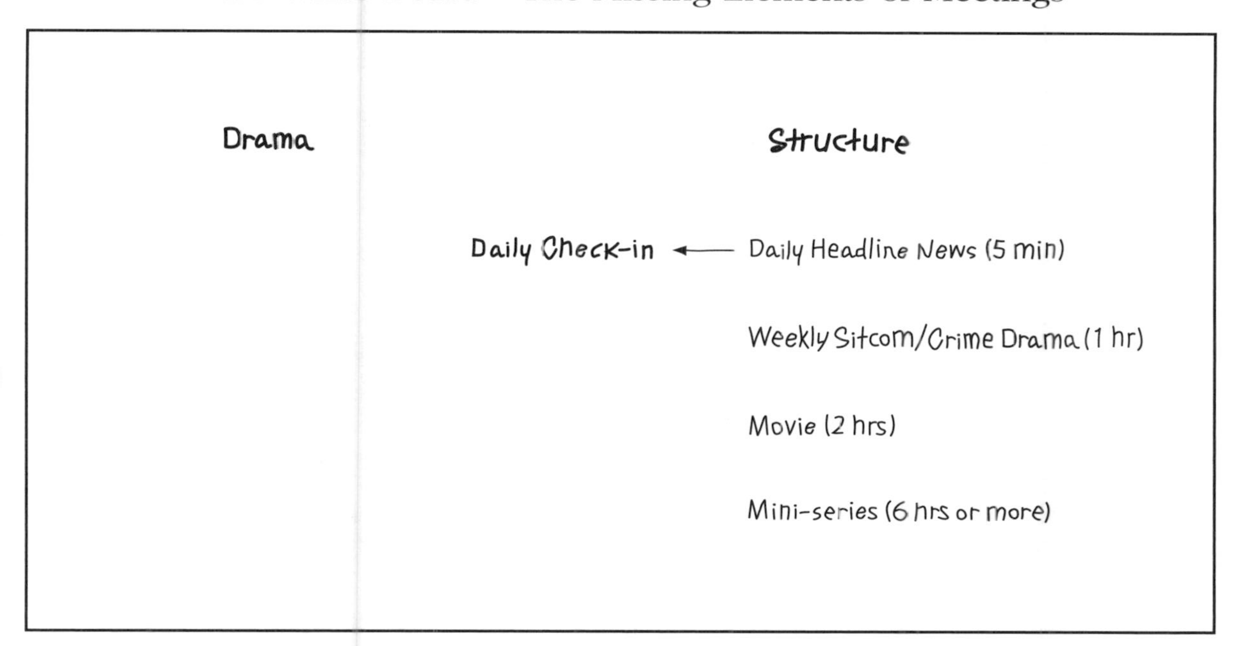

Casey asked the next question. "But what about people being out of the office? It isn't realistic or feasible to do this every day, is it?"

Will thought about it for a second. "Well, even if there are only three of you in the office on a given day, you should probably still have the Daily Check-in meeting. Because if you think about it, even that would make a difference. For one, those three people would be on the same page. And better yet, if one of the other team members called from the road and wanted to know what someone was doing, any of you could answer them. And remember, we're only talking about five stinking minutes. Maybe I'm wrong, but I can't believe that you are all so efficient that you couldn't possibly spare five minutes."

The nods around the table indicated that everyone seemed to be on board. Except for Matt, who wasn't ready to concede just yet. "What makes you think we'll have anything to say to each other every day?"

Will was waiting for that question. "Well, if you don't, then it will be a fifteen-second meeting. But I'll bet you the seven bucks in my pocket that a bigger challenge will be keeping the sessions to five minutes or less. Which is critical, by the way. Because you don't want them turning into daily staff meetings."

Even Tim was nodding now. "Okay, keep going. What about the sitcoms and crime dramas?"

Will took a breath. *One meeting down, three to go.*

THE WEEKLY TACTICAL

"Let's talk about our staff meetings. These should be the sitcoms or crime dramas of meetings. They take place once a week, same bat time, same bat channel."

Will was glad to see that they all understood his *Batman* reference.

"With a sitcom, you generally know what you can expect, how long it's going to last, and you can count on a guaranteed resolution. Not overly exciting maybe, and it's not going to change your life. But it's consistent, predictable, and ultimately satisfying."

"I'm not following you." Casey was determined to understand what Will was saying.

Will decided to be as literal as possible, not wanting to lose the importance of his message in the analogy. "Okay, the weekly staff meeting should be focused exclusively on tactical issues. And it should run like clockwork, lasting approximately sixty minutes, maybe less." He paused before delivering the most controversial point of all. "And there is no agenda."

Connor jumped in before Casey could. "What? Isn't that going to make the meetings worse than they are now?"

"No. They'll be exponentially better. Here's why." He paused for a moment before explaining. "These Weekly Tactical meetings will start with everyone giving a sixty-second report about what they're working on that week." At that point Will wrote *Weekly Tactical* on the board.

"Like the lightning round on a game show," remarked Casey.

Will smiled. "Right, like the lightning round. I like that. Anyway, it's nothing more than going around the table and asking every person at the meeting to report on the three primary activities that are on their plate for the week. And everyone gets only one minute."

Nervous laughter filled the room as everyone contemplated having to condense their remarks to sixty seconds.

"Only one minute?" Matt questioned.

Before Will could answer, Connor raised his hand. Will noticed that he was smiling, so he called on him.

"I have a question for you, Will." He paused. "Where in the world did you get all of this stuff?"

The focus in the room suddenly shifted from analytical curiosity about meetings to personal curiosity about Will.

Sophia chimed in, smiling warmly. "I've been wondering the same thing myself."

Will was caught off guard. "I don't know."

He was hoping they would let the question die.

"Come on. You had to learn this stuff somewhere." Connor wanted an answer.

Will's White Board—The Missing Elements of Meetings

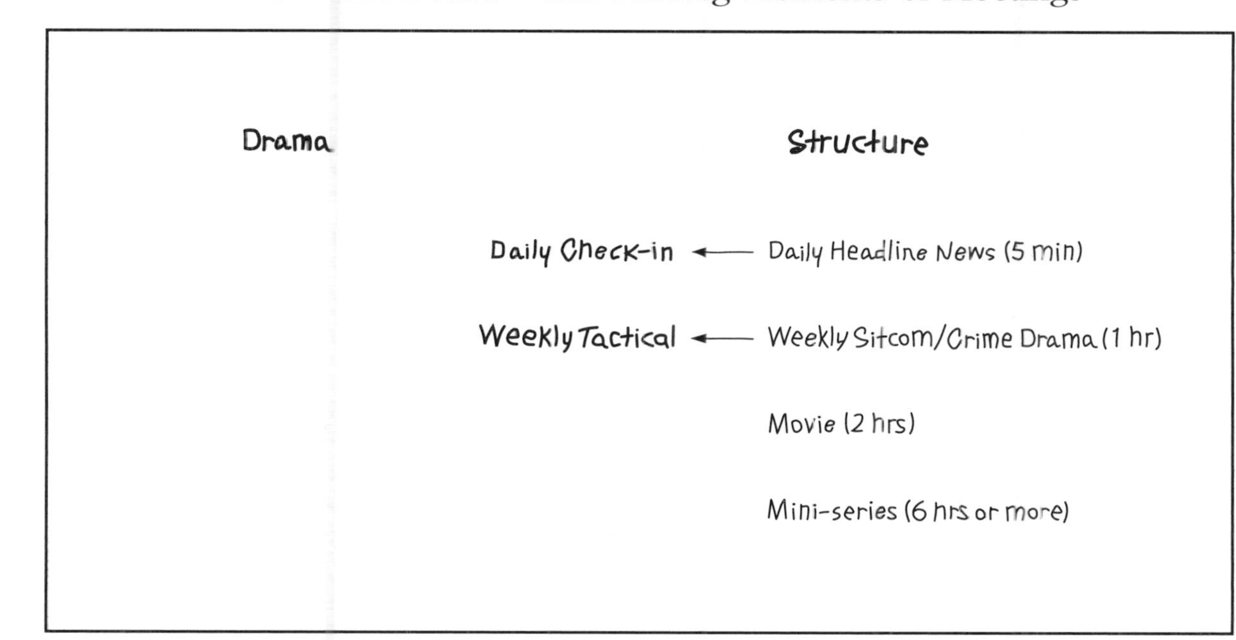

Will took a breath. "Well, I suppose my mom has something to do with it. She's been an executive for years, and she's good at this kind of stuff." He hesitated, searching for a more compelling answer. "And I guess I just find it interesting."

For a few moments, the team seemed to be collectively examining Will, as though he were a novelty item, or a precocious little brother.

Will wanted desperately to deflect the attention from himself. "Matt, you asked a question about whether one minute was enough for the lightning round?"

Matt nodded. "Yeah. It takes us longer than that to agree on lunch."

"Okay, let's test my theory." Will looked around the room and settled on Tim. "What are the three things that you're doing this week?" Will looked down at his watch to time him.

Tim was suddenly pressed. "I don't know. Let me see. There's the budget meeting on Thursday. I have a lot to do for that." He paused, thinking. "I'm meeting with a few new law firms to see if we should make a change to reduce expenses. What else?" he asked himself. "Oh. I'm doing a facilities planning session to see if we need to find extra space across the street."

"What law firms are you talking to?" Will asked.

"Everardo, Dibay and Galvez out of Carmel. And Carlson, Beans and Schultz from San Jose."

Will looked down at his watch. "That took just thirty-seven seconds, and you didn't even have time to prepare. And on top of that, I asked a follow-up question for clarification."

Based on the looks on the faces of the people seated around the table, Will decided he had made his point successfully. So he pushed on.

"Once everyone has reported in, which for us would be a grand total of seven minutes, then, and only then, should we put together an agenda. Because we would then know what was actually going on in the organization. It doesn't make sense for Casey, or anyone else, to try to guess at what we should be talking about during these Weekly Tactical meetings until they know what people are actually doing."

Casey looked skeptical. Will noticed this and called him out. "What's wrong?"

Casey thought for a moment. "I think you're missing something." He paused, still thinking. "Before you put together the agenda, I think you need more information than just everyone's activity lists."

Will prodded him. "Like what?"

"Well, I think you'd also need a score card or a progress report of some kind. You'd want to know where the organization stands relative to its near-term goals before deciding what needs to be talked about during the meeting. Maybe four or six key metrics. Not too many, but just enough to give us a snapshot."

Matt was nodding now. "That makes sense. But which metrics?"

Casey was thinking out loud now. "I don't know. Revenue and expenses for sure. Maybe product development status. And key account penetration. That's probably all we'd need."

Will asked, "How long would that take to review?"

"Ten minutes," Casey replied. "Maybe even five."

Will now understood Casey's point. "Okay, I get it. If we set the agenda based solely on our activities, but without understanding the metrics, we might not know where to focus. Maybe something is going on that no one has on their radar screen."

Michelle weighed in now. "I'm just wondering if there is anything else we would want to know. Like employee turnover or advertising effectiveness."

Casey shook his head. "I don't think so. I think too much information would only distract us." He smiled. "Which is ironic for me to say given the way meetings are run now."

Will couldn't have been happier with the input from Casey and his team, and he didn't want to lose momentum. "So let's get back to the weekly meeting. After less than fifteen minutes, everyone in the room would know what everyone else was doing, and where the company stood against key goals." He paused for effect. "And then we could figure out what we should discuss for the rest of the meeting."

"How would that work?" Michelle asked.

Will shrugged and answered. "Well, I guess Casey would say, 'Okay, now that we know what's going on and how we're doing in general, what do we need to talk about today so that we can make as much progress as possible this week?' I think the right topics would naturally rise to the surface."

"That just seems so counter-intuitive." Tim was still having a hard time accepting that agendas would be eliminated. "I've always heard that pre-set agendas and timely minutes were the keys to great meetings."

Will shrugged. "Well, I'm no expert, but I haven't been to any good meetings, here or anywhere else. So I don't see why we should be following conventional wisdom at this point. And I don't think J.T. Harrison is going to give you any slack for doing it by the book."

Will could tell by Casey's reaction that he had said something controversial. And then it dawned on him that he had slipped, momentarily forgetting that no one else knew about Harrison's criticism of the meetings, nor his implied threats.

Michelle was confused. "What do you mean by that?"

Will decided his best chance to divert the conversation away from Harrison was to dive deeper into the topic. "I mean, I don't understand how a person could possibly predict the right topics for a tactical meeting, not to mention the priorities of those topics, without first hearing about what was actually going on."

Michelle wasn't so easily diverted. "Yeah, you already said that. But what does that have to do with J.T. Harrison?"

Will looked at Casey, and wanted to crawl into a hole.

OUT OF THE BAG

Casey sighed hard, and took a deep breath. "You guys might as well know. J.T. thinks our meetings—my meetings—are terrible. And he's pretty much implied that my job is on the line because of it."

Naturally, Tim responded first. "That is the most ridiculous thing I've ever—"

Casey interrupted. "I know. I know. But it doesn't matter. The fact is, Wade Justin lets Harrison do pretty much whatever he wants, and this is what he wants to do."

The room sagged as everyone digested the news and began pondering its potential implications.

"And besides," continued Casey, "you yourselves said the meetings are horrible."

Connor jumped in. "Yeah, but we just meant that they're not as—"

Casey held up his hand to interrupt again. Connor and the rest of the room went quiet. "Regardless of J.T. Harrison and his ego, I think we need to fix these damn things. For the good of the company."

Will wanted to crawl out of his hole and hug his boss.

Then Matt spoke. As usual, he glossed over the emotional context of the situation and brought it back to practical issues. "I have a question about these weekly tactical staff meetings, or whatever you call them. After the first part, the lightning round, how in the world do you keep the discussions to forty-five minutes or less?"

Will was glad to get back on topic. And he had been waiting for someone to ask that question. "You do it by limiting the conversation to topics that have an immediate impact on tactical issues and goals."

"Okay, professor boy." It was Tim, and he was clearly teasing. "What happens when someone suddenly decides they want to solve world hunger during a staff meeting, or even come up with the next brilliant game idea?"

Will smiled. "Aha. That brings us to the next program." He stood and walked toward the board. Before he could get there, Sophia interrupted.

"Can we take a quick break? Connor and I have a five-minute call with the PGA office. I don't want us to miss any of this."

Casey nodded his approval and announced, "Okay, let's be back here in ten minutes. Not eleven. Ten."

Everyone broke for the doors, except Matt, who came up to Casey to tell him how much he disliked J.T. Harrison. When he was gone, Casey turned to Will.

"I hope we can pull this off." He smiled, but in a desperate sort of way.

G2

More determined—and worried—than ever now, Will decided to use the ten-minute break to do some research. He went to his cubicle and called one of his new friends in the company, Maddie Peyton, an administrative assistant to one of Playsoft's other division heads.

Relieved that he caught her at her desk, Will didn't waste any time. "Hey Maddie, it's Will Petersen calling from Monterey. I have a quick favor to ask you."

"Alright. But first, is it beautiful in Monterey today? I have to know."

Will looked outside. "Actually, it's a little overcast."

"Good," she said. "Because it's raining here in Chicago and I don't want to hear that it's another day in paradise out there."

They laughed.

"What can I do for you, Will?"

"First, I wanted to let you know that I'll be in Chicago tomorrow to help with the game conference."

"Great. I finally get to meet you in person."

"Yeah. I'll track you down tomorrow afternoon. But I'm

calling for another reason." He hesitated. "This is going to sound like an odd question, but what do you know about J.T. Harrison? He's the head of—"

Maddie interrupted. "Yeah, I know who J.T. is. Why do you ask?"

Will had to be evasive. "Well, I met him last week and he comes over here from time to time, and I'm trying to get a handle on him, that's all." There was silence on the other end, so Will continued, "I heard he has a reputation."

Finally Maddie spoke, but the tone of her voice was suddenly a little less friendly. Not hostile, but detached. "Well, I've met him a few times myself. Right after the merger he came to Chicago about once a month to see Nick. He seemed alright to me."

Will could tell she was holding back. "Does Nick get along with him? Did he like spending time with J.T.?"

Maddie paused, her voice much quieter now, but back to being friendly. "Look, Will. I'm going to be as honest with you as I can. Those first few months after the merger were horrible. I almost quit the company. And Nick did too."

"And I'm assuming that it had something to do with J.T." Will didn't have enough time to be more subtle.

"Okay, here's the only thing I can say about the experience. Nick made me swear not to tell."

Will could hardly contain himself. "Okay, go ahead."

"No," she said. "That's it."

"What do you mean?"

"I mean, I had to promise Nick that I wouldn't say anything about what happened. That's all I can tell you. You'll have to draw your own conclusions."

Will felt like he was talking to someone in a witness protection program. "One more question, Maddie."

"Go ahead."

"What made Nick stay?" Before she could respond, he threw in another: "And how do they get along now?"

Maddie chuckled, though quietly. "Hey, you said *one* question."

"Sorry, I lied."

"Will, I like you."

He knew she meant it.

"And that's why it's so hard to tell you that I can't tell you. I'm really sorry."

Will accepted her apology and assured her that he understood. And then, wanting to defuse a little of the heaviness of their conversation, he teased her. "Hey, suddenly the clouds have broken and it's gorgeous outside. It's like another day in paradise."

Maddie laughed. "You brat."

Will thanked her, and said good-bye.

What is going on around here? he wondered.

THE MONTHLY STRATEGIC

When Will returned to the conference room upstairs, everyone was just sitting down. Immediately he noticed a change in the atmosphere. More serious. More intense.

Casey spoke first. "Okay everyone, let's get on with this." He looked at Will.

"Alright. On last week's episode—" everyone laughed at Will's TV humor—"Matt asked the question about how to limit discussion during the Weekly Tacticals to forty-five minutes. Which was a perfect lead-in to our next type of meeting. The Monthly Strategic."

He went to the board and wrote it down beneath *Daily Check-in* and *Weekly Tactical.*

"When you're in the middle of a Weekly Tactical and someone says, 'Hey, let's talk about that new competitor in our market' or 'I think we should look into a joint venture with ESPN' or 'Let's rethink our advertising strategy,' that's the moment where you have to resist the urge."

"The urge?" Matt wanted clarification.

Will's White Board—The Missing Elements of Meetings

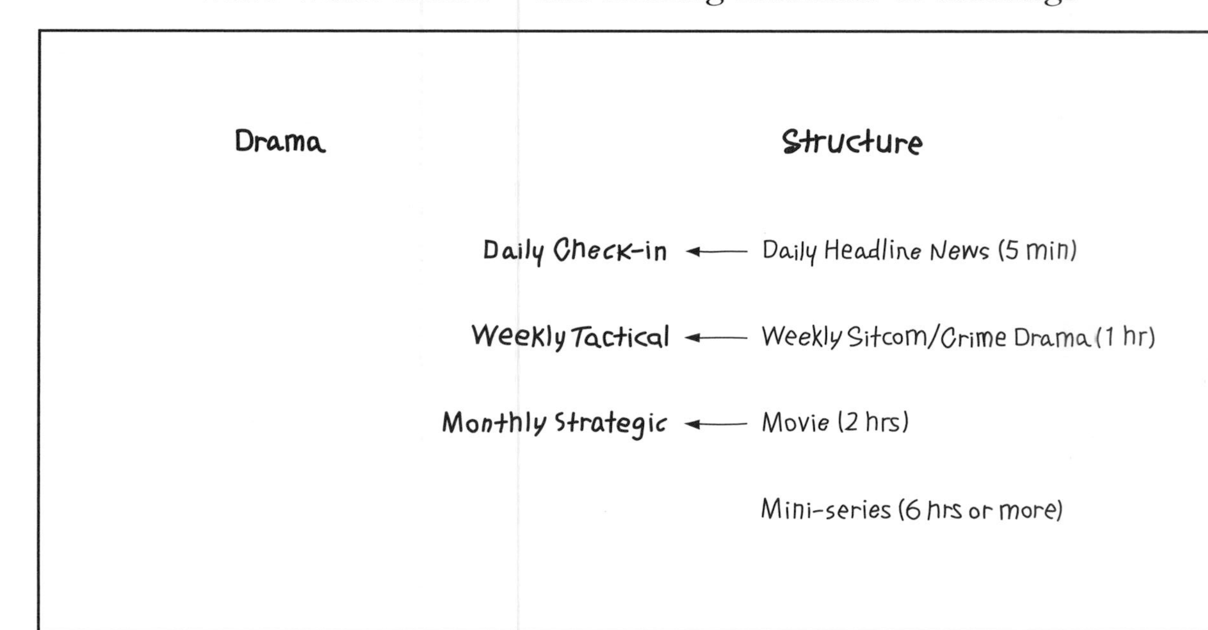

"Yeah, the urge to go off on some terribly interesting and important conversation that has no real impact on your ability to accomplish your near-term goals."

Sophia confessed, "But those are the only—" She caught herself, "I mean those are the best parts of the meeting."

Everyone laughed at her near slip.

"And that's the point!" Will was animated again. "Those are definitely the most interesting topics. They are the reasons you go into business in the first place. To engage in discussions where you can use your analytical skills, your experience, and your intuition to solve a big problem."

"Right, so what's wrong with talking about them during the Weekly Tacticals?" Sophia persisted.

"There are a couple of problems. And they're huge."

Will again had everyone's attention.

"First, you don't have enough time during your staff meetings to completely dive into a big issue. So the conversation ends up being incomplete, anecdotal, hurried, and ultimately unsatisfying."

He paused to give anyone a chance to disagree. They didn't, so he went on. "Second, even if you did have enough time, it's almost impossible for people to shift mindset from a tactical issue to a strategic one."

Casey added, "This is the contextual thing I was talking about before."

"Right." Will wasn't sure everyone was understanding this one, so he used an analogy. "Imagine having two television sets side by side and trying to watch *Driving Miss Daisy* and *Everybody Loves Raymond* at the same time."

Everyone seemed to enjoy the analogy, but it wasn't enough. "Or imagine the president of the United States discussing the White House Christmas Tree lighting ceremony in the same meeting where the topic of terrorism or national defense was being considered. It just makes no sense."

Casey took a deep breath and spoke, as though he were realizing the futility of what he'd been doing for so long. "And trying to deal with strategic issues during the weekly meetings usually means you get distracted and don't deal with any of the short-term issues that you really need to resolve if you're going to keep the business moving."

That hit a nerve with Tim. "Exactly! We get so off track with what's going to happen next quarter or next year that we don't really come to any conclusions about what we should be doing next week. Or even tomorrow, for that matter!"

Everyone smiled at their unrefined but suddenly passionate CFO.

Will didn't want to lose the momentum. "And that's why you need to have the self-control to table those interesting, long-term strategic issues until you have enough time to give them the attention they deserve."

Casey suddenly had a question. "But what if you can't wait until your next Monthly Strategic? An issue might need more immediate attention."

"No problem." Will was loving this. *Maybe I should be a professor,* he thought for a nanosecond. "If the issue can't wait, then have a Monthly Strategic that evening. Call it," he paused to think about it, "an Ad Hoc Strategic. I don't know. Just don't confuse it with the Weekly Tactical."

Casey nodded and wrote down Will's answer.

"I have a question." It was Matt. "How many topics can you take on during these Monthly Strategics?"

Will didn't hesitate. "One or two. Maybe three if you set aside enough time. The key is to pick the right ones, and really get your hands around them."

"So then you should have an agenda for these meetings?" Tim seemed to have a thing for agendas.

"The answer is yes. Absolutely. Agendas are critical for these meetings because you might need to prepare for them by doing a little research. And you want people thinking about the topic ahead of time. That will make the quality of the debate much higher, and reduce the anecdotal nature of so many meetings like these."

Michelle raised her hand. "You said two or three hours. What happened to keeping the meeting to two?"

Will thought about it for a second. "Well, the Daily Check-in and the Weekly Tactical should be strictly timed. But Monthly Strategics are different."

He paused, considering something. It was clear that Will was refining his theories as he spoke. "You know, sitcoms always have to be thirty minutes. If one day your favorite show went on for forty-five minutes, you'd be confused. But movies are different. You don't go to a movie thinking, 'Okay, give me exactly ninety-three minutes of entertainment.' Heck, some of the best movies are long ones. And then again, some of them are short. I just don't think you should over-manage the time you spend during Monthly or Ad Hoc Strategics. In fact, I think you should probably carve out a big chunk of time, like four hours, just in case you want to keep talking."

"Four hours?" objected Tim.

Casey came to the rescue. "You know, I heard a story the other day about Microsoft and the fact that their executive team will sometimes have meetings that go on late at night, or even into the next morning."

Will nodded. "You see, these strategic meetings are going to be so engaging, so compelling, that the time will become unimportant. Before you know it, three or four hours will have flown by."

"When are we supposed to get our work done?" Matt was suddenly frustrated.

Much to Will's delight, Casey now seemed to be taking over the class. "Okay, Matt. What in the world could be more important for the executive team to be dealing with than the three sample issues I raised? What were they? A joint venture, a new competitive threat. . . . " He paused, trying to think of the third topic.

Michelle remembered. "A new marketing strategy."

Matt was nodding his head as if to acknowledge his boss's point.

Michelle drove it home. "And besides, who cares how long it takes if you're making a decision that you're going to have to live with for years?"

Tim laughed, as if something had just occurred to him. "Yeah, I don't care how long a movie is, as long as it's interesting. I've seen *Braveheart* five times. In fact, I once saw it twice in two days. That's more than six hours of sitting on my butt in a dark room, and I was ready to go a third time the next day, but I couldn't convince anyone to come with me."

Sophia couldn't resist an opportunity to tease her CFO. "You've seen *Braveheart* five times, but you haven't seen *The*

Sound of Music or *The Godfather?* You're a strange, strange man, Tim."

He laughed.

Connor put the discussion back on track with a question. "How do you decide what topics to discuss at the Monthly Strategic?"

Will rejoined the conversation. "The best place to find topics will probably be the Weekly Tactical. When someone raises an issue that is too big and hairy you'll just parking-lot it on a list for the next monthly meeting."

Connor continued. "But you're probably going to have a lot of topics. How do you decide which ones make the cut?"

Casey handled this one. "I have a feeling that the most important ones will be fairly obvious. And if they aren't, we would probably just debate about it for a few minutes to see who could make the most convincing argument. But I don't think there's any scientific solution. It's a judgment call."

As tired as he should have been, Will was feeling energized again. The group had completely engaged in the conversation, and Casey seemed to have regained some of his confidence. And Will couldn't deny feeling a sense of relief that his theories seemed to be making sense.

But as confident as he was feeling about getting the group to understand his model, Will was also starting to wonder if it would be possible for them to implement it before J.T. took whatever action he was planning to take.

DIRECTING FOR DRAMA

Casey pushed on, determined to figure this out. "Okay, so you have an agenda with two or three items on it."

"But remember, even one is okay," Will reminded him. "Sometimes only one really matters, and you have to have the discipline to limit yourself to it."

"Right. Anyway, how do you structure the meeting itself?"

Will smiled. "Now we get back to my movie analogy. Remember, this is the feature film. And the key to making it great is. . . ."

He paused, hoping someone would finish his sentence.

Of all people, it was Matt. "Conflict."

"Right. This is the meeting that is most like a feature-length movie. And the leaders of these meetings have to think of themselves as directors. Get people hooked in those first ten minutes, then mine for ideological conflict, and drive it to conclusion."

Every member of the team was taking notes now.

Emboldened by their buy-in, Will pushed on. "Is anyone up for talking about the last type of meeting? I think I've already used up my thirty minutes."

The group seemed to take a collective breath, and nod their approval. Casey agreed.

Will went back to the board, suddenly feeling exhausted. *Hang on,* he told himself. *You're almost there.*

THE QUARTERLY OFF-SITE REVIEW

Will didn't have the energy for more analogies, so he got straight to the point. "Okay, the last meeting that you need to have is the Quarterly Off-Site Review." He wrote the words on the board.

Tim weighed in. "We already have those. Not always quarterly, but a couple times a year we have off-sites."

Will had heard about their off-sites. So he prodded Tim, like Columbo questioning a guilty suspect. "What do you usually do at these sessions?"

Tim looked around for help. Sophia obliged. "We usually go away for a night or two, maybe to San Francisco, or Napa, or Tahoe."

"And when you're there, what happens?"

"We spend the morning talking business, then go skiing, or wine tasting, and then have a nice dinner. And sometimes we bring our spouses."

Connor chimed in. "And we've done some team building. Like the ropes course, and the human pyramid thing."

Will's White Board—The Missing Elements of Meetings

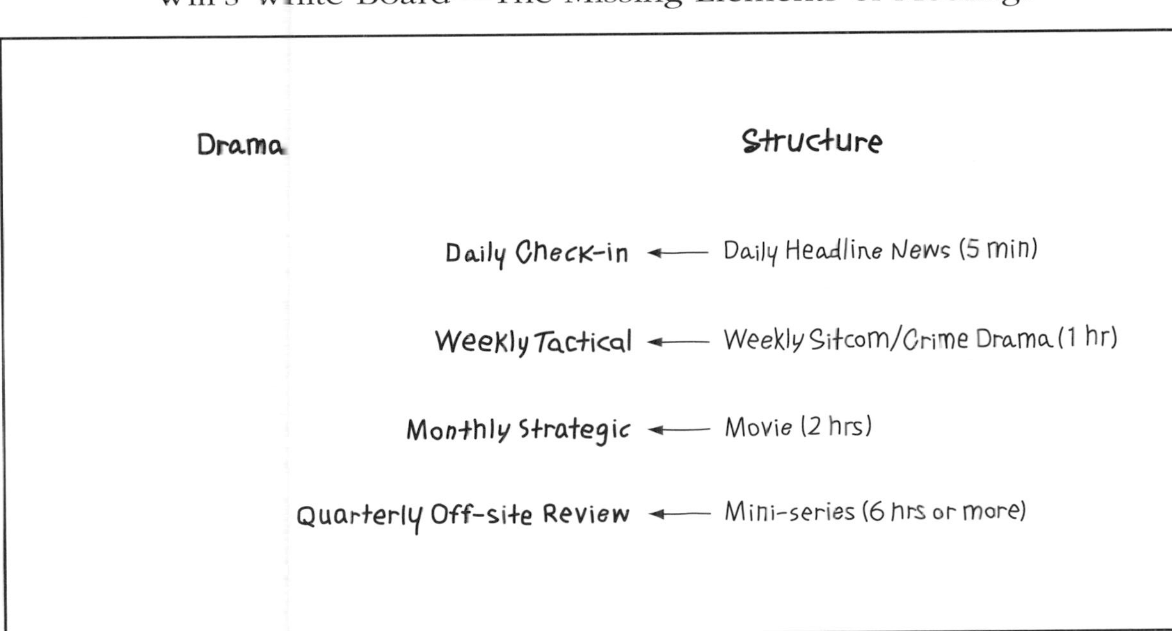

Everyone groaned as they remembered the silly exercises.

"So what exactly do you talk about during the business part of the meeting?"

Everyone in the room seemed to shrug simultaneously. Casey took a stab. "We cover some of the same issues as the weekly staff meeting. And we talk about goals for the next year. Sales targets. Margins. Things like that."

Will was ready to pounce. But gently. "Okay, I don't know a heck of a lot about off-sites. But I know a pretty decent executive—"

Connor interrupted to tease Will. "Are talking about your mommy?"

The room howled.

Will smiled sheepishly. "Okay, yes, it's my mom."

They laughed.

Casey informed them, "The thing you should know about Will's mom is that for eight years she ran all of operations at the automobile plant in Fremont. She is a shrewd, tough executive."

Sufficiently embarrassed now, Will continued. "Anyway, she refers to those kinds of meetings as boondoggles. And she thinks they are a terrible waste."

Michelle countered. "I have to disagree. I think that executives who spend time away from their families and make sacrifices in their lives need to spend some time away from work, getting to know one another's spouses, and dealing with each other in a more personal, social way. I think it's worth the cost."

Will seemed surprised by Michelle's comment. "She never said that off-sites like that were a waste of money. She said they're a waste of an opportunity to have some of the most critical conversations that an executive team must have."

"What do you mean?" Michelle wanted to know.

"The Quarterly Off-Site Review is a critical chance to step back from the daily, weekly, monthly grind, and review things from a distance."

"Review what?"

For the first time, Will read directly from his notes. "Well, strategy. The competitive landscape. Morale. The dynamics of the executive team. Top performers. Bottom performers. Customer satisfaction. Pretty much everything that has a long-term impact on the success of the company. Stuff you just can't cover in weekly or monthly meetings."

Matt asked the usual question, but this time he couched it in gentler terms. "Now, I'm not saying these aren't important. But how much time do you need for a Quarterly Off-Site Review?"

Will hesitated. "I'm not sure."

Casey was. "Based on the list of things we would need to cover, I'd say two days."

Matt winced.

"But if you stop and think about it, that's just eight days a year. Out of how many total work days? Two hundred and forty? That's a whopping 3 percent."

"Still," Matt persisted. "Two days?"

Casey was now a convert. "Yeah. Two days to figure out who our best people are, and how to manage the stragglers up or out. Two days to figure out what GoBox and Gamestar are doing. Two days to give each other some feedback. Two days to figure out if our strategy still makes sense."

Sophia had now drunk the Kool-Aid. "And, again, what else are we doing that is more important than that?" She laughed out loud. "I don't know about the rest of you, but I'm sitting here embarrassed that we're not doing this already."

Everyone, even Matt now, seemed to agree.

Casey raised his hand and spoke. "I don't know about you guys, but I think it would be hard for me to take part in these meetings and play the role of facilitator. What does everyone think about having a consultant help out?"

"Are you talking about just the Quarterly Off-Site Reviews, or all of them?" Connor asked.

"Well, I was thinking about the off-sites, but maybe we should think about the others too."

Michelle spoke up first. "I think that getting help with the quarterly meetings would be okay. As long as the person was a good fit, and wasn't trying to prove how smart he was."

Heads nodded as everyone thought about bad facilitators they had known.

"I know a guy who is amazing at that," Casey reported with passion. "He takes the time to learn the business, but he doesn't insert himself into everything. He just helps, in an almost invisible way."

Will wanted a little more clarity. "What about the other meetings?"

Michelle shook her head. "I don't think so. The daily and weekly meetings certainly don't need facilitation, other than from Casey. And the monthly meetings, I don't know. It seems like we'd be constantly trying to educate someone from the outside."

Matt agreed. "Yeah. It would be better to have someone on the inside do it. Someone like Will."

No one said anything, but every person in the room understood the magnitude of what their skeptical colleague had just done. For him to acknowledge that Will was adding value was huge.

Casey looked at his watch, and then at Will. "This seems like a good time to get back to our original agenda." His remark was more of a question for Will than a statement.

Will could have continued, but was more than happy to end on a high note. "Yeah, I think so too. We've pretty much covered the four kinds of meetings." As the conversation shifted, Will felt relieved. He only wished he had more confidence that Casey and his team could actually employ these ideas while he was gone, and most important, in time for The Meeting.

CHICAGO HAZE

Two days later, Will found himself walking the Navy Pier on Lake Michigan at midnight, confused and depressed. Was it that he gave Casey just a fifty-fifty chance at surviving the next few weeks? Or that he was starting to wonder what the next step in his own career should be? Or that he was the world's best-educated trade show carpenter?

Whatever the case, he didn't like feeling out of control. Not one to let himself flounder for long, Will considered his options.

If he stayed in Chicago for another week, as was the plan, he would go crazy. More important, Casey would struggle to implement the new meeting plan and maybe get it wrong.

If he left Chicago early, he would put a few of his new trade show colleagues in a slightly difficult position. And he might even upset Casey.

But then again, he reasoned, *if it's a matter of saving Casey's job, then it's worth the risk.*

The next morning Will was on a plane headed for California.

PART FIVE

Resolution

NOTHING TO LOSE

Casey was gone when Will arrived at his office late that afternoon. So he went to his cubicle and began to assemble a document outlining his theory about meetings. Will was determined to drill the ideas into Casey and his team so that, by the time J.T. and Wade arrived the following week, it would be easy for them to stick to the plan.

Still waiting for Casey, Will began to feel uncomfortable about how he would explain having left Chicago. On the other hand, he reasoned, he didn't really need this job. *So they fire me. I can still help Casey get ready for the meeting.*

But would they let him? Would Casey let him? *"How did I get in this situation?"* he wondered to himself out loud.

"What situation?"

It was Casey, and his question startled Will, who almost fell out of his chair.

He tried to recover. "I didn't see you there. You scared me."

Casey modified the question. "What's going on, Will?"

Will stood up. "Let's talk about this privately."

They went into Casey's office and shut the door.

Before Casey could sit down, Will launched into his speech. "Okay, here's the deal. I don't care about this job."

Casey looked puzzled.

Will quickly explained. "I mean, I actually care about it a lot. But I don't care if you fire me. I just want to help *you* avoid getting fired."

Casey was moved and amused by the passionate statement of concern, but a little unnerved by the explicit description of his dire situation. Somehow things felt better when no one actually verbalized the potentially horrible outcome.

Will didn't wait for Casey to respond. "Listen, you deserve to hold onto this company. And if one stupid meeting is going to determine whether or not that happens, then why the hell should I sit in Chicago straightening out brochures and handing out glow-in-the-dark paperweights to technology reporters?"

"What difference does it make, Will? Don't you think he's already made up his mind?" Casey seemed angry now, in a desperate way, but not at his temporary assistant.

"I don't." Will didn't know if he really believed that, but felt that Casey needed to hear it. "And even if there is only a slight chance that we can change his mind, then don't you want to make sure we make the most of it?"

Will's words seemed to jolt his boss. Unsurprisingly, given the similarities in their looks and mannerisms, it reminded Casey of the way that Ken Petersen used to lecture him on the golf course.

Casey nodded slowly. "So what did you have in mind?"

CRAMMING

For the next few hours, Will and Casey reviewed the meeting document that Will had put together, speculated about the mindsets of J.T. and Wade, and discussed the probable challenges that the team would have in pulling off the looming meeting.

It was Casey who asked the most important question. "So what type of meeting is it going to be?"

Jet-lagged and hungry, Will didn't seem to understand the question.

Casey explained. "Is it a Weekly Tactical, a Monthly Strategic, or a Quarterly Off-Site Review? It's certainly not a Daily Check-in."

Will thought for a moment. "I think it has to be a—"

Casey interrupted. "A Monthly Strategic."

Will nodded, glad to see that he and his boss were on the same page. "I agree," he said, "but tell me what your thinking is."

"Well, we've got two or three hours, and that fits with the monthly meeting. More important, though, we're not going to make much of an impression on J.T. by doing the lightning round and the metric review."

Will was starting to believe that they might be able to pull this off.

Casey continued. "We're going to need to dive hard into some meaningful issues, and show him that we have the passion and rigor that he's probably looking for."

Two things occurred to Will at that moment. First, Casey had indeed understood and bought into the theory. Second, he seemed to have moved beyond being mad at J.T. He just wanted to win.

Sufficiently hungry now, Will and Casey left the office and went to Cannery Row to have dinner. They spent the next two hours trying to decide which issues should make the cut.

SCRIMMAGE

The next morning Casey called a special meeting of all his direct reports. Matt and Tim protested, having already set their schedules for the day. Uncharacteristically, Casey simply told them to move things around and to be on time.

When everyone had arrived in the board room, Casey began.

"The purpose of this meeting, oddly enough, is to talk about another meeting. As you know, next week J.T. and Wade will be here to observe our staff meeting. And as you also know, I'm under a little pressure, it seems. But I don't want to talk about that anymore."

The executives looked at one another, confused.

Casey explained. "What I mean is that we have to forget about any consequences or concerns we have about what the future holds, because we just don't have any control over that." He paused. "Other than making next week's meeting the best one we've ever had."

The faces around the table seemed to clue in now.

Tim was the first to comment. "So, we're here to talk about what to say next week, and how to position things." It was a statement, but Casey knew he meant it as a question.

"No. I want to be very clear about this. Next week is not a performance. We're not going to rehearse. Instead, we're going to prepare, and then we'll go in there and push each other like we've never pushed before."

The room suddenly came to life. Will decided it was part excitement, part fear.

Matt raised his hand. "What exactly does that mean?"

"I'm not sure yet. And that's the point. Today we'll decide what our agenda looks like, and then we'll go do whatever research we need so that by next week, we'll come back ready to rock and roll."

Everyone laughed at Casey's new and unnatural bravado.

"Rock and roll?" Connor could not resist teasing his boss.

Casey smiled, comfortable joining his team in making fun of him. "Okay, maybe that's not exactly my style."

Will was again reminded why he liked this man so much.

Casey continued. "But the point is the same nonetheless. We are going to be ready to have a raw, dramatic, and effective Monthly Strategic meeting."

Tim frowned. "So we're not doing the lightning round, and all that stuff?"

Casey shook his head. "Nope. This is a strategic meeting. And we'll be limited to two topics. And we need to decide right now what they should be."

The team seemed to be waiting for someone to go first, so Will threw out an idea. "Everybody write down one issue that you think would be good for next week."

The executives spent the better part of a minute thinking and writing, and Casey called for their responses.

Matt: Next product
Sophia: Expansion into mainstream video games
Michelle: Competitive acquisition
Tim: Hiring freeze for non-sales positions
Connor: Forty percent salary increases for the executive team

Connor couldn't help making a joke. But he did have a serious idea.

Connor: Shifting advertising budget to sponsorship of a PGA golf tournament

"Okay," Will explained, "before we vote, I want everyone to give us a sixty-second pitch about why you think your idea should make the cut."

For the next ten minutes or so, the executives advocated their topics, at times pushing one another for clarification. Finally, when they had finished, Casey called the question. "Everybody has two votes. You can use them both for one idea, or split them between two. But you can't vote for your own idea."

After the vote, there were two clear favorites: expansion into mainstream video games and PGA golf tournament sponsorship.

Casey announced, "So these are our topics. We all had a chance to weigh in, so let's not go back and try to second-guess ourselves. What we need to do now is go out and do whatever research we need so that by next week we are prepared to drive the discussions to closure. Any questions?"

No one seemed to have one, until Tim raised his hand. "Yeah, I think we should appoint someone to be in charge of each topic, in terms of organizing the research and teeing up the topics next week."

"That's a great idea." Casey agreed. "Connor, I think it makes sense for you to take the PGA sponsorship topic, and Sophia, you do the game expansion. Why don't you each take a first pass at research requirements, and then we'll talk tomorrow during our Daily Check-in about dividing things up."

He paused. "Okay, everyone, let's get back to work."

As the team broke for the doors, Will wondered, *Is this the same company I joined two months ago?*

RESEARCH

For the next week, Connor, Sophia, and their colleagues—divided now into teams—allocated a good portion of their time to reviewing sales figures, looking back at previous budgets, and doing informal surveys of selected vendors and customers.

Other than attending the Daily Check-ins, Casey stayed out of the work, wanting to maintain a sense of neutrality so that he could be as unbiased and incisive as possible come Monday. Instead, he and Will spent time talking about the role Casey would need to play at the meeting.

Aside from the research itself, something interesting was happening to the team as they prepared for the big day. Their morale began to rise slightly.

On numerous occasions Sophia and Connor ordered dinner brought into the office so their respective teams could stay and hammer out their findings. Hallway interaction between executives—and their staffs, who had become involved in the research—increased. A spontaneous contest even broke out among a few employees as to who could be first to uncover a piece of competitive information.

Though barely discernible to the naked eye, the office had definitely changed as a result of the collective activity. Still, none of the employees knew about the unpleasant fear that had provoked the call to action.

On Friday afternoon, Casey called the team to his office for a quick conversation. He was surprised to find that their enthusiasm had disappeared.

"What's wrong with you guys?" Casey asked.

Sophia went first. "Well, I can't speak for Connor's team, but we thought we would be on the same page by now. We're as divided now as we were before all this started."

Connor was nodding. "I'd say that's partially true for us too. But more than that, we're afraid that our data is inconclusive. We don't think we could make a solid recommendation by Monday."

"I think you guys have lost sight of what you've been doing." Casey then smiled. "I don't care if you don't have a concrete suggestion. And it doesn't bother me at all that you aren't agreeing about the right decisions. In fact, I would be concerned if you were."

They were confused, so he went on.

"That's the whole purpose of the meeting. I can't wait to go in there and argue about things, and to have some real data to test our arguments against. But at the end of the day, there is no spreadsheet or calculation that will make the decisions for us. It eventually comes down to a judgment call. And that's the fun part."

Casey had done a good job of masking any fears he maintained about Monday's meeting. And he definitely had some.

"Okay, then, I'll see you all on Monday. Let's be ready to go."

Though he had certainly diminished some of the concerns that his executives had brought with them to the meeting, there was no denying the nostalgic sense of dread that filled the room at that moment.

Will decided that they were all thinking the same thing. *Is this going to be our last meeting?*

PRE-GAME

On Monday, Casey woke up at dawn and had no chance of going back to sleep. What he didn't know was that he could have called Will, because he was up too, almost as anxious as his boss.

By seven thirty, Casey was sitting at his desk, not sure what to do. Ten minutes later Will arrived. He headed straight for Casey's office.

Casey greeted him with an announcement. "He's not coming."

Will was shocked. "J.T.?"

"No, Wade. His assistant left me a voice mail at five thirty this morning."

"What did she say?"

"Just that he decided he had other priorities and probably wouldn't be able to make it."

"That's good news, right?" Will was hopeful.

"It would have been, except she said that J.T. would still be coming, and that Wade had full confidence in J.T.'s judgment."

Will wanted to tell Casey not to worry, that her message was actually a positive sign. But he didn't want to insult his boss's intelligence.

For the next half hour, the two friends talked about everything but the meeting. In fact, they didn't talk about business at all. They discussed Monterey, their families, their churches, current events, golf, the weather—everything but the company. Will was glad to provide a distraction. He knew that there was nothing else Casey could do to prepare for that morning, other than relax.

But just as he did when he was golfing professionally, Casey started to feel the pressure. No matter how loose a golfer feels before a tournament, when the time comes to hit that first shot off the tee, even the most confident player feels some pressure. And with fifteen minutes to go before the meeting, Casey was not feeling too confident. He politely asked Will to leave him alone for a while.

For the next ten minutes, Casey sat in his office and wondered what it would be like to have to leave his office for the last time. He was now so nervous he thought he might be sick. *What did I do wrong?* he asked himself. He called his wife, but she wasn't answering at home or on her cell phone. *How did I let this happen?*

Before Casey could spiral any deeper, Connor and Sophia entered the office. It was five minutes to ten. They had come to escort their boss upstairs.

THE MEETING

When they arrived, J.T. was already seated, but he didn't acknowledge anyone in the room. He was talking on his cell phone and seemed remarkably upbeat.

When everyone took their seats at ten o'clock sharp, J.T. enthusiastically ended his remarks to the listener on the other end of the line: "Listen, I've got to go. Yeah, it was great talking to you too. Thanks. Bye."

Will hoped that J.T.'s demeanor would continue into the meeting, and that it was a good indication of what to expect for the next two hours. It wasn't.

Closing his phone, J.T. turned toward Casey and made eye contact for the first time. His positive disposition seemed to have suddenly disappeared. "Good morning," he said, neither warmly nor coldly.

Casey responded in kind, and kicked off the meeting. "Okay, we have two topics to discuss and two hours to discuss them, so let's get started. Why don't you go first, Sophia?"

Sophia cleared her throat. She seemed more nervous than anyone had ever seen her. "The question we looked at was whether or not we should start making more traditional games, appealing to the kind of kids who represent the fastest growth segment in the market."

Casey didn't wait for her to continue. "So what would you recommend?"

Sophia looked at him, surprised. She stammered. "Well, as I mentioned to you on Friday, I'm not sure that—"

Casey interrupted. "I know. But if you had to make a recommendation right now, what would it be? There's no right answer. I just want to know where you stand."

Sophia seemed to have no confidence in her answer. "Well, I guess I'd say we should look at some new games with more mass market appeal, but not go too far in diluting our brand."

Casey smiled, and then challenged his head of sales. "Come on, Sophia. You're not running for office. Should we expand or not?"

Sophia didn't know what to say. She looked at her team.

Tim tried to bail her out. "Okay, I was on the project team with Sophia, but we didn't necessarily agree. Personally, I don't think we should expand, not just because of our market dilution, but because it would put us in a position of competing with other Playsoft divisions."

"Who cares?" It was Will.

Casey was suddenly worried that his assistant was going to launch into yet another mild tirade. But he decided that trying to intervene would probably make matters worse. So he pushed for an explanation.

"What do you mean?"

Will took a breath. "What I mean is, we're going to be evaluated as a division, and that means we have to demonstrate revenue and market share growth as a division. As long as the company judges our performance that way, we have to run our business that way."

No one actually turned their head toward him, but everyone in the room snuck an unassuming glance at J.T. to see how he would respond. Everyone but Casey, who pushed for debate.

"Anyone agree with Will?"

The room was silent, aside from the scratching of J.T.'s pen as he took notes.

Sophia spoke up again. "I do. I say we have to do what we have to do."

Casey was unfazed by the potentially controversial discussion. "Okay, I want to hear from everyone on this. But I'll be up front about where I stand as of—" he looked at his watch, "seven minutes after ten. I'm not in favor of this kind of expansion. But not because of the potential internal competition. As long as the company looks at its financials in a purely divisional manner, then I think Will and Sophia are correct. By the way, I hope this changes and we start taking a more holistic, one-company view sometime in the future."

J.T. was writing faster now.

Casey continued. "My opposition to the expansion is based on maintaining a clear competitive outlook and brand position. I just believe that if we lose our focus, we become like everyone else. And then we have no advantage at all."

Now Tim weighed in. "But the numbers say we should do this. The mass market will grow at 15 percent over the next five years. Our niche market will get 2, maybe 3 percent."

"But how many more initiatives can we take on?" It was

Matt. "I know you've heard me say this before, but I'm concerned that we won't be able to sustain our current levels of quality."

"Michelle?" Casey looked toward his head of HR. "What do you think?"

She was mortified. "I don't know. From an employee standpoint, I think some people would be excited. Others would be very disappointed. Particularly the old-timers." Michelle then made a request that blew everyone away. "I'd like to hear what J.T. thinks about it."

Now everyone in the room turned toward their visitor as though they were at a tennis match and the ball had just been hit to him.

J.T. continued writing until he finished his sentence, and then looked up from his pad. "I have no idea."

"Come on, you must have some thoughts about this."

Casey was sure that it was Will who would have made the remark, and so was surprised that it had again come from Michelle. The team looked at her as if she were throwing herself on a grenade.

But rather than an explosion, something worse happened. "No, I really don't," J.T. responded without emotion, and continued writing.

Casey was remarkably unflustered. "Alright then. It looks like we have a decision to make here, folks. Someone tell me what the worst thing that could happen would be if we decide to expand."

For the next forty-five minutes the group speculated on worst-case scenarios, best-case scenarios, and competitive responses to each possible decision. They looked at sales figures from the past four quarters, projections for the next two, and analyst reports about what the industry was likely to do.

And they argued. Back and forth, sometimes with data, other times with nothing but intuition. Every member of the team spoke out, some of them changing their opinions when presented with new perspectives or information. Sophia and Matt turned out to be the strongest advocates on either side of the issue.

Finally, when the discussion seemed to have run its course, Casey called the question. "Okay, we could take another six weeks to do more research and analysis, but I don't think that's necessary. We've been living in this market for years, and we've assembled quite a bit of information here. I think we know all we need to know to make this decision."

He then looked around the room. "Okay, this isn't a democracy, but I'd like to know where everyone stands." They each weighed in.

Connor:	No expansion.
Matt:	No expansion.
Tim:	Expansion.
Michelle:	No expansion.
Sophia:	Expansion.

Casey then turned to Will. "What about you?"

Will hesitated and seemed slightly embarrassed. "I didn't think I'd be voting."

Casey smiled. "Well, you heard everything we did. If you were in our shoes, what would you do?"

Will surprised everyone with his answer. "I'd probably expand."

Casey then looked at J.T. for his input. He shook his head to say *nothing from me.*

Casey nodded and looked around the room as though he were mentally sifting through the various opinions. "Okay. I have to admit that I've changed my mind twice in the past hour. But I'm feeling pretty strong about this decision. And everyone here needs to support it regardless of how you voted."

He looked at Matt and Sophia. "Are we okay with that?"

They nodded emphatically.

"We are not going to expand. In fact, we're going to cut a few games out of our portfolio."

A few eyebrows around the table went up.

"Instead, we're going to focus on stealing share from our competitors in our primary markets, and solidifying our position against potential new competitors. And forgive the terrible cliché, but that means we have to get leaner, and yes, we have to get a little meaner. If we do this right, I think we could see 4 percent revenue growth, and more than 10 percent increase in profits."

The room digested his remarks.

Casey continued. "But it will not be easy. And we're going to have to make some changes in our culture."

"Like what?" Michelle wanted to know.

Sophia answered before Casey could. "Like fewer people doing more work."

"Which means working more hours." Connor chimed in.

"It's about time." It was Tim who said it. As soon as it came out he looked like he wanted to take it back.

Casey pushed. "You want to expand on that?"

Tim paused and smiled. "Not really."

Everyone laughed.

"But I think you're going to make me, so I will. I don't want to be overly harsh about it. Not that I would be."

Everyone laughed again at Tim's sarcasm.

"I just think that things have gotten a little soft around here. That's all. And I suppose in the past that was okay. But now that we're part of a public company, people could probably stand to feel a little more of the pressure that a public company feels. And now's the right time to make the change."

Heads around the table were nodding.

Casey moved the meeting along. "Okay, we'll schedule another strategic meeting to decide which products to cut, and how to move forward. Sophia, would you work with Will to make that happen sometime this week?"

She nodded and took a note.

"Okay, Connor. Let's talk about PGA sponsorship."

It was at that moment that J.T. raised his hand. "I have a question." He looked at Casey. "What do your numbers look like over the past month?"

Casey froze, like a deer staring into headlights. Will wanted to jump up and shake him.

J.T. started to repeat the question, but Casey calmly interrupted him. "I heard the question. But today's meeting is about strategy. We talk about numbers and metrics at our Weekly Tactical meeting."

"Excuse me?" J.T. was not flinching.

Casey wasn't sure whether J.T. was upset at him for not answering his initial question, or whether he was unclear about the distinction between strategic and tactical meetings.

Casey chose the latter. "Our Weekly Tactical meeting. That's where we review our numbers, find out what everyone's doing, and solve tactical problems so we can keep moving forward."

He paused, and when J.T. didn't respond, Casey continued. "You see, today's a strategic meeting, which means we're going to stick to two topics and wrestle them to the ground."

Now J.T. tensed up a little. "Well, do you think you could humor me and show me what your sales look like?"

Sophia was just about to jump in and give the man what he wanted, but before she could get a word out of her mouth, Casey responded.

"Sure, J.T. But we'll have to do it after the meeting. We've only got two hours here, and we need to use every minute." He smiled graciously, and with absolutely no hint of defensiveness or condescension on his face. Then he said, "I hope that's okay."

For the next three and a half seconds, the air in the room seemed to disappear. No one breathed. And then, just as J.T. seemed like he was about to challenge Casey, he picked up his pen and started writing again.

Will would later tell his mother that what Casey had done was one of the most subtly impressive things he had ever seen.

Casey then turned to his head of marketing, unfazed. "Okay, Connor. What do you have for us?"

Connor didn't speak right away, but instead waited to see if the averted encounter was really over. When it was clear J.T. had backed down, he began.

"Okay, we did some analysis to compare the effectiveness of our print advertising with the sponsorship of a PGA tournament. And while we didn't come to any definitive answers, we were surprised to find that sponsorship is not as expensive as we had expected."

Tim couldn't resist a discussion about expenses. "How much does it cost?"

Connor cleared his throat. "Somewhere between two and three hundred grand."

Tim laughed out loud. "And that's not expensive?"

Connor defended his statement. "Not when you look at our current advertising budget. I mean, it's certainly more money, but the issue is how effective would it be."

Sophia had now sufficiently recovered from Casey's exchange with J.T., and she joined the discussion. "Don't get me wrong. I'd love to see us get some attention from more golfers and pro shops. But the thought of actually reducing advertising terrifies me."

"Why?" Connor asked.

"Come on, Connor. You and I are constantly complaining about not having enough air cover out there. If we disappear from the radar, aren't we just inviting our new competitors to step into our spot?"

Will challenged Sophia. "You're assuming that our current advertising is effective. How confident are you about that?"

"Not very confident at all. But I don't see anyone else pulling back on advertising, and so I'd hate to be the only one."

And then J.T. spoke up. "How are you currently assessing advertising impact?" To everyone's surprise—and relief—there seemed to be no apparent motive behind the question. No challenge. No skepticism. Just curiosity.

Connor responded, as comfortably as though he were talking to Tim. "We trace as many orders as we can back to advertising sources, but we don't get enough of them to call it a valid sample."

"Why is that?" J.T. wanted to know.

Sophia responded. "Not enough people buy the game directly from us, either on-line or over the phone. Most of our sales come from pro shops and retail stores. We don't have enough contact with buyers."

Just a hint of J.T.'s arrogance seemed to resurface suddenly. "I don't get it. Why don't you just do a customer survey? Or have your retailers do it at the point of sale?"

Sophia explained with confidence. "We've done that. But there are two problems. First, pro shops look at us like we're Martians when we ask them to do surveys. They're not exactly into customer analysis. I mean, they're pumping out green fees, sweaters, hot dogs, and hard-boiled eggs, all in one pop."

Casey shook his head and smiled. "Yeah, and their margins on hot dogs are a hell of a lot bigger than on games."

Everyone, including J.T., laughed.

Sophia continued. "The second problem is that so many of the people we do survey tell us they heard about our games from a friend. That's one of the wonderful curses of having a product that spreads through word of mouth."

J.T. seemed almost satisfied with Sophia's rationale.

Tim brought the discussion back to earth. "Regardless of all that, I still don't see how we could consider spending so much money on a single event. I mean, what if it rains that day?"

Casey fielded the question. "Thc thing is, it's not really a single event. I mean, there is so much advertising for a tournament in advance, and so much coverage around the country for the five days leading up to and following the event, that it amounts to a pretty sizable push."

Will jumped in now. "It's kind of like Enterprise Rental Car."

Everyone suddenly turned toward Will, who hadn't said much until that moment. They seemed confused.

"You know. Enterprise." He repeated.

Connor recited the company's tagline. "Call Enterprise. We'll pick you up." Everyone recognized the ad, and chuckled at their jovial head of marketing.

Will went on. "Yeah, everyone knows their tag line. The thing is, when I worked in advertising, I remember hearing that a huge percentage of their media budget went into one event: the NCAA basketball tournament. They did a long-term deal with the NCAA years ago, which everyone thought was too expensive. And now, from that one source, they generate almost all of their brand awareness."

Heads around the table nodded. Except Matt's.

Casey looked at his engineer. "What are you thinking over there?"

Surprisingly, Matt didn't bite. "Nothing. Sounds good to me."

Casey knew him better than that. "Come on, Matt. What would you say if I told you we were going to cut everyone's

IT budgets by 5 percent in order to sponsor the Greater Bakersfield Open?"

Suddenly Matt sat up in his chair. "Okay, I admit I don't like this idea. I mean, you can't use the NCAA tournament as an example, because you're talking about one of the most popular events in the country. And one that goes on for a month."

Connor responded quickly, if not testily. "True. But we're not talking about a product that needs to be marketed to the whole world. We know our customers. And most of them are pretty serious fans of golf. And have you seen the ratings for tournaments lately? Come on, we have to have some guts here."

Maybe it was because J.T. was in the room. Or maybe Matt was just in a bad mood. Whatever the reason, he didn't react well to Connor's response. "Guts? I think we need more analysis, and less guts. And besides, what happens to our guts when Tiger pulls out of the tournament the week before?"

The tone of Matt's voice stalled the discussion.

Casey smiled big. "Now this is the kind of passion I want to hear."

That was just enough permission for Connor to defuse the situation. In what appeared to be a completely serious, even combative tone, he announced, "Okay, Matt. You want to decide this analytically." And then he made the rock, paper, scissors motion with his hands.

Matt laughed, and the rest of the room followed suit.

Connor followed his stunt with a real point. "The thing is, Matt, I'm betting that Enterprise couldn't scientifically justify their NCAA decision. I mean, let's do all the analysis we can, but in the end we're going to have to pull up and shoot."

Matt slowly nodded his head. "Now I know why I didn't go into marketing."

Everyone smiled at their technologist.

"But let's not get ahead of ourselves here. I think there is a lot more analysis we can do before we have to rely on intuition." It was Michelle. "I'd like to know how this decision will be impacted by the one we made earlier today."

Sophia wasn't following her. "What do you mean?"

"Well, if we cut back the number of games we distribute, doesn't that have an impact on how we advertise?"

Connor nodded. "Absolutely. I mean, if we move into croquet and other sports—"

Tim interrupted, sarcastically. "Don't forget archery. Hey, maybe we should sponsor an archery tournament?"

Even Connor laughed at the joke, which was directed at him. "Yes, even archery. But if we move into those sports, we'll need to do more mass market advertising. But if we consolidate more around golf, the sponsorship route will become more attractive."

"That's a good point." Casey acknowledged. "It would be great to focus our messaging and our product development. And I'd have to think there would be some economies of scale there."

Sophia asked a question, but directed it to the entire room. "So, should this decision drive which games we choose to ditch, or should the games we ditch drive this one?"

The room was momentarily dazed by the profound question. Before anyone could weigh in, a cell phone rang.

In addition to ensuring that his meetings would always end on time, the only other issue that Casey had insisted on was that no one bring cell phones to meetings. That meant it had to be J.T.'s.

Their guest immediately looked down to see who was calling. Then, he opened the phone, spun around in his chair, and spoke in a tone that was only slightly quieter than normal.

No one spoke during the ensuing brief conversation, more out of curiosity than courtesy.

"Hey there."

J.T. listened for a moment.

"No, I'm in a meeting. What's up?"

After another moment.

"No. Not right now. I'll call you from my car. Bye."

J.T. closed his phone, grabbed his notebook and jacket, and stood up. "Excuse me. Gotta go."

Without so much as looking at Casey, he left the room.

No one spoke for five complete seconds.

And then Tim spoke. "See you next time, Gordon Gecko."

It took a beat for the room to digest what the CFO had said, and then the place howled. Partly because of Tim's reference to the slimy executive from the movie *Wall Street,* and partly out of nervous relief.

Casey was the first to stop laughing. "Okay, let's finish this discussion."

The room slowly quieted, until Matt added dryly. "Except he looks more like Captain Kirk."

The fact that it came from Matt made it funny. That it was true made it hilarious. There was little chance of reining the group in now, so Casey called a break. "Let's be back here in ten minutes."

LETDOWN

The surreal atmosphere that existed before the break was long gone by the time everyone returned. Will felt like a baseball player in the seventh game of the World Series, having the game cancelled because the lights went out. There was no satisfaction. No closure. And worse yet, a possibly devastating outcome ahead of them.

If Casey was feeling any of that, he wasn't letting on. "Okay, where does everyone stand on the sponsorship question?"

No one responded immediately. Finally, Connor spoke. "Don't you think we ought to talk about what just happened?"

Casey didn't hesitate. "Not right now. Like I told J.T., we have two hours to get through this, and we haven't come to a decision about the sponsorship issue yet."

No one doubted Casey's sincerity. And just like that, the conversation shifted back to business. For the next hour, the team debated the issue without distraction. In the end, they decided that sponsorship made sense, and that the next step would be to start talking to tournaments looking for advertisers.

And when it became clear that the meeting was almost over, the noise in the room diminished considerably, but no one wanted to leave.

Casey pierced the awkward moment. “I don’t think I’m exaggerating when I say this was a good meeting.”

Everyone agreed.

“And I think we shouldn’t worry too much about what happens next. I mean, in terms of J.T. Harrison and all of that.” He paused. “I know that’s easier said than done, but there’s no use worrying about it now.” Casey then smiled. “Who’s up for lunch?”

Not coincidentally, everyone was available.

FRIENDLY FIRE

After returning from lunch, which at times felt like a going-away party, Casey found himself feeling oddly at peace with his situation. Even defiant. *If they're dumb enough to fire me, then they deserve what they get,* he declared silently.

And then the phone rang. It was Nick, the head of Playsoft's on-line gaming division in Chicago.

"I'm calling to find out if you know anything about a rumor I just heard from a mole at corporate."

Casey suddenly wished he'd let the call go to voice mail. But he liked Nick, so he played along. "I'm all ears."

"Well, evidently there's going to be some sort of organizational announcement tomorrow. And guess who it involves?"

After deciding that Nick could not possibly be thinking of him—no one would be so cruel to make such a call—Casey started to wonder. "Let me guess. J.T. Harrison."

Nick was genuinely surprised by Casey's answer. "So I guess you're tied into the rumor mill, too?"

"No. I just had a hunch." Casey considered telling Nick what he'd been going through, but decided he didn't need to relive the ordeal yet again.

After a few minutes of banter, the call ended, and Casey's confidence had vanished. In a perfect world, he would have thrown himself into his work as a matter of principle. But he had done more than his share of being strong for the day, and decided to find his wife and enjoy the rest of the afternoon with her.

It was the last time he mentioned or thought about J.T. Harrison that day. Which made the next morning all the more shocking.

THE ANNOUNCEMENT

Casey came to work neither early nor late. He quickly made his way through the halls, not wanting to run into any of the employees whose cubicles were located between the front door and his office. He was in no mood for small talk.

When he approached his office, there was no sign of his assistant, though in fact, Will had already arrived. Will would later admit that he had purposefully avoided running into Casey that morning.

Casey went to his desk, said a silent prayer, turned on his computer and opened his e-mail. And there it was.

To: All General Managers and Vice Presidents
From: Wade Justin
Subject: Organizational Change (time-sensitive and confidential)

(Note: This message is for General Managers and Vice Presidents only. Please keep the contents confidential until three o'clock today, when a general message will be distributed to all employees.)

This is a difficult announcement for me to make, because it marks the end of many years of hard work. Effective immediately, I will be leaving my position as Chief Executive Officer of Playsoft, though I'll be staying on as Chairman of the Board. This is a move I've been postponing for the past two years, but it's the right thing to do for me personally, and for the organization.

I am pleased to announce that the new CEO will be J.T. Harrison. For those of you who don't know J.T., and even for those of you who do, I'd like to tell you about him.

J.T. has been with Playsoft for nine years. For the past five of those years, he has been focused on strategies for growing the company, and he is responsible for most of the acquisitions we've made during that time.

But unlike so many M&A executives, J.T. has played another key role in the acquisition process, one that has been critical to the success of our company. And he has done so without acknowledgment or fanfare. Until now.

You see, each time Playsoft has acquired a new company, J.T. has taken responsibility for challenging the new organization to dramatically improve its performance in whatever area he sees it lacking. And notwithstanding the recent challenges in the stock market, the results of J.T.'s work have been nothing short of staggering. Playsoft has consistently acquired companies and watched their sales increase by an average of 25 percent during the first two years after the merger. Most recently, he engineered the deal with Yip, and we're looking for big things from our colleagues in Monterey.

Unfortunately, in the course of his work, J.T. has had to ruffle the feathers of many of the leaders in our various divisions, all for good reason. I am relieved to be able to reveal his role so that people throughout the organization who might have seen J.T. in a somewhat controversial light can finally see him as the selfless and dedicated leader that he really is.

Please join me in welcoming J.T. to his new role. And please accept my gratitude for the years of hard work that so many of you have given to Playsoft and our many divisions.

Yours,
Wade Justin
Former CEO, Still Chairman of the Board
Playsoft

And there it was. Casey struggled to sort out his feelings at that moment. Relief. Anger. Disbelief. Exhaustion. Mostly relief that he now understood what J.T. had been up to.

The first thing he did was call his wife and fill her in. Then he went out to look for Will. He found him sitting at his desk now, smiling hesitantly.

Right away Casey knew that Will had seen the e-mail. He smiled and shook his head. "This is one strange company."

They laughed.

CLOSED LOOP

At five minutes to five, Casey considered going home early. The past few days had been some of the most emotionally draining of his career, and he decided nine holes of golf would be a perfect antidote.

As he gathered his paperwork and turned off his computer, he was startled by a visitor. "Where are you going?"

It was J.T. Harrison. He was standing in the doorway of Casey's office, looking serious.

Casey hesitated, and then replied, "Golfing. Want to come?"

J.T. shut the door behind himself. The two executives sat down.

Casey's new boss spoke first. "This is always the hardest part for me."

"What part is that?" Casey was confused.

"Apologizing. Or not apologizing. I mean, I know how hard the last few months have been for you, and I'm sorry for that. But there was a method to my madness."

Casey studied J.T. He said nothing.

J.T. broke the silence, smiling. "Do you have any questions for me? You can have a free shot, with no retribution."

"So did you just make up the meeting thing to push me?"

J.T. suddenly stopped smiling. "No way. I was completely serious about it. I mean, I wasn't expecting to have to replace you, but I was genuinely concerned about your meetings." He paused. "I still am. But yesterday was definitely better."

"You really think it was that big of a deal?" Casey seemed to be shedding any animosity and was now more curious than anything else.

Nodding his head, J.T. defended himself. "Absolutely. I learned early in my career as a consultant that bad meetings at the executive level usually indicated a huge gap between performance and potential. And, Casey, your meetings were really horrible."

Casey smiled, accepting the criticism with humility. "Did the other division heads go through the same thing I did?"

"Yeah. But not about meetings. DeStefano had a problem with performance management. Nick struggled with expenses. Those aren't your issues. As far as I can tell, you're a good manager, and you keep a relatively tight control over expenses."

Casey shook his head as he digested the situation. He couldn't deny that he was starting to warm up to the company's new CEO.

J.T. went on. "By the way, you probably shouldn't tell anyone what we're talking about."

"Why not?"

"Two reasons. First, if I ever have to do it again with another new VP, they'll know what's going on and it won't work." J.T. smiled at the thought. "But there's a more important reason. By now your staff is probably pretty pumped up by the tension of the past few weeks. If they find out it was partially manufactured, they'll lose some steam."

Casey didn't necessarily like what he was hearing, but decided it was the right thing to do.

J.T. seemed to be reading his mind. "And remember, Casey, I'm serious when I say 'partially manufactured,' because this was not just smoke and mirrors. If you had completely whiffed on the meeting issue and showed no progress at all, I would have started thinking about my next steps. Just because I do this with all new division heads doesn't mean it's not real."

At that moment Casey decided that J.T. Harrison's intentions had been good, and that despite his rough personality, he was a stand-up guy. "You sure you don't want to play some golf?"

"I'd love to. Really. But I've got to get back to San Jose for a meeting with investor relations tonight."

Casey seemed surprised. "You mean you came over here to have a fifteen-minute conversation with me?"

"No." J.T. answered matter-of-factly. "I thought it would take five or ten."

The two men smiled, and before another thirty seconds had passed, J.T. was out the door.

A half hour later Casey was teeing off.

FALLOUT

Immediately after reading Wade Justin's note, Casey's team was in shock that J.T. would be the new CEO of their company. But they quickly shifted into relief mode when their boss informed them that he seemed to be out of the woods, from a career standpoint.

As a result of the sudden amnesty, the sense of passion and energy among the team, and the employees who worked for them, increased dramatically. More important, it proved to be sustainable. Which was remarkable considering that few people at Yip knew what had really happened during that fateful summer.

For the next month or so, Will worked closely with Casey's team to fully implement the meeting structure. At times they struggled as executives occasionally tried to skip a meeting here or there. But Casey wouldn't relent, and within a few months, the daily and weekly meetings began to grow roots in the culture.

The strategic meetings were another story. At first, the team had too many of them, reacting to every new issue by scheduling another meeting. Eventually, however, they learned to distinguish between topics that could be addressed by a subset of the team, and those that were truly critical to the entire organization.

By Halloween, the group had completed their first Quarterly Off-Site Review, and they were all surprised to find it to be not only interesting, but one of the most productive two days they had ever spent as a team. Matt even admitted that he was looking forward to the next one.

Within just a few more weeks, each of the four meetings had been tweaked and adjusted, and the entire system was working smoothly. And while that was good for Casey and the company, it wasn't great for Will, who had suddenly lost his sense of meaning and interest.

It was then that Will realized he would either have to leave the company earlier than expected or take a real job there and make a go of a career in software. Which wasn't such a stretch, given Will's background in media.

But Will wasn't about to let go of his passion, not yet. So he resigned just before Thanksgiving, after finding Casey a suitable replacement, and moved back to Southern California to begin his next adventure in film and television.

FAST-FORWARD

As so often happens, Will and Casey dove into their own busy worlds and didn't keep in contact with one another as often as they had assured each other they would. Eventually they lost track of what was happening in each other's careers and lives.

And then one Saturday they ran into each other in San Francisco, in the pro shop at the Presidio Golf Course near the Golden Gate Bridge. Casey was there to play a round with an old friend, and Will was with his dad. The CEO of Yip had little trouble rearranging the tee times so that the two groups could play as a foursome.

After the first nine holes. Casey and Will swapped partners so they could share a cart for a while, and catch up on things.

Will learned that Yip was still a division of Playsoft. The company within a company had solidified its position in its market, and was growing slowly but profitably. Playsoft was doing fine too, but J.T. was no longer CEO.

Will was surprised. "What happened?"

"After a year, he decided to step down."

"Was he forced out?" Will wondered out loud.

"Not at all. In fact, they tried to keep him. But he just didn't like being CEO. 'Too much maintenance,' he said. So he started a consulting firm that parachutes into troubled companies to shake things up."

Will laughed. "Perfect."

Casey went on to update his former assistant about the status of his staff, including the two new executives on his team. He told Will about the sales of Yip's various products, and about the success of Yip's golf sponsorships.

As much as he enjoyed hearing about all that, there was one thing that Will really wanted to know. "How are the meetings?"

"Oh, we stopped having them." Casey said as he lined up a putt.

Will's jaw dropped. "What?"

"Yeah, we just e-mail each other about decisions now. It's a lot more efficient." Casey drained the putt, and then looked up at Will. He was smiling.

"So that was a joke? Please tell me it was a joke."

Casey laughed. "Of course it was. Don't worry, we're still doing the meetings. And pretty much the way you helped us set them up. You should have been there when the newer members of our team first joined, though. They thought we were crazy with all the conflict and drama. But they love it now."

As Casey stood next to Will and watched his old friend and mentor, Ken Petersen, putt the ball, he became suddenly overwhelmed by what these two men, father and son, had done for him.

Not knowing how to express his emotions at that moment, he simply put a fatherly arm on Will's shoulder. And said nothing.

The Model

THE PARADOX OF MEETINGS

Meetings are a puzzling paradox.

On one hand, they are critical. Meetings are the activity at the center of every organization.

On the other hand, they are painful. Frustratingly long and seemingly pointless.

The good news is that there is nothing inherent about meetings that makes them bad, and so it is entirely possible to transform them into compelling, productive, and fun activities. The bad news is that in order to do this, we will have to fundamentally rethink much of the way we perceive and manage meetings.

That means we cannot keep hating them. And we must abandon our search for technological solutions that will somehow free us from having to sit down face to face. And we have to stop focusing on agendas and minutes and rules, and accept the fact that bad meetings start with the attitudes and approaches of the people who lead and take part in them.

The best news of all: for those organizations that can make the leap from painful meetings to productive ones, the rewards are enormous. Higher morale, faster and better decisions, and inevitably, greater results.

The purpose of this section is to provide a brief summary of my meeting theory so you can implement all or part of it within your organization, and reap some of those rewards.

EXECUTIVE SUMMARY

The first question that needs to be asked and answered about meetings is this: What is the real problem? Actually, there are two.

First, meetings are boring. They are tedious, unengaging, and dry. Even if people had nothing else to do with their time, the monotony of sitting through an uninspired staff meeting, conference call, or two-day off-site would have to rank right up there with the most painful activities of modern business culture. And when we consider that most of the people struggling through those meetings do indeed have other things to do, that pain is only amplified.

Second, and even more important, meetings are ineffective. The most justifiable reason to loathe meetings is that they don't contribute to the success of our organizations. With so many demands on people's time, it is especially frustrating to have to invest energy and hours in any activity that doesn't yield a commensurate return.

So the big question is *why?* Why are meetings boring and ineffective?

Meetings are boring because they lack drama. Or conflict. This is a shame because most meetings have plenty of potential for drama, which is essential for keeping human beings engaged. Unfortunately, rather than mining for that golden conflict, most leaders of meetings seem to be focused on avoiding tension and ending their meetings on time. And while these may seem like noble pursuits, they lie at the heart of bad meetings.

To make meetings less boring, leaders must look for legitimate reasons to provoke and uncover relevant, constructive ideological conflict. By doing so, they'll keep people engaged, which leads to more passionate discussions, and ultimately, to better decisions.

Meetings are ineffective because they lack contextual structure. Too many organizations have only one kind of regular meeting, often called a staff meeting. Either once a week or twice a month, people get together for two or three hours of randomly focused discussion about everything from strategy to tactics, from administrivia to culture. Because there is no clarity around what topics are appropriate, there is no clear context for the various discussions that take place. In the end, little is decided because the participants have a hard time figuring out whether they're supposed to be debating, voting, brainstorming, weighing in, or just listening.

To make our meetings more effective, we need to have multiple types of meetings, and clearly distinguish between the various purposes, formats, and timing of those meetings.

The remainder of this section provides a more complete discussion of the two underlying problems with meetings—

lack of drama and lack of structure. It also includes tangible solutions for addressing them, as well as warnings about the challenges that can often get in the way.

PROBLEM #1: LACK OF DRAMA

Meetings are not inherently boring. By definition, they are dynamic interactions involving groups of people discussing topics that are relevant to their livelihoods. So why are they so often dull? Because we eliminate the one element that is required to make any human activity interesting: conflict.

I took a screenwriting class in college and, as a hobby, have written a few screenplays myself. In the process of my study and practice of the craft, I learned something about drama that I believe is completely relevant to meetings.

You see, conflict is at the center of every great movie. It is the essence of drama, and it is the reason audiences become and remain engaged in a story. And whatever type of conflict it is—man versus man (Luke Skywalker and Darth Vader in *Star Wars*), man versus nature (Chief Brody and the shark in *Jaws*), man versus himself (John Nash struggling with his mental illness in *A Beautiful Mind*)—without it we lose interest.

But what do movies and meetings have to do with one another? Think about it this way. Most movies are written to be approximately two hours in length, give or take twenty minutes or so. Many of our meetings go for about two hours, give or take twenty minutes.

Now imagine if I were to ask a room full of executives which they enjoy more: meetings or movies? They would probably think I was joking. And yet, meetings should be more interesting than movies because they have more inherent potential for passion and engagement than movies do. I realize that this will sound preposterous if you've turned straight to this chapter without reading about Yip Software first, so let me explain why I believe this to be true.

MEETINGS VERSUS MOVIES

First, meetings are interactive, movies are not. You can interrupt someone during a meeting and say, "I think you should reconsider your decision. . . . " But you can't interrupt an actor on the screen and say, "Don't go into the house, you knucklehead. You're going to get your head lopped off!" When you go to a movie, you are a passive observer, not a participant.

Second, meetings are directly relevant to our lives, movies are not. Decisions made during a meeting have an impact on how we will spend our time and energy in the immediate future. At the end of the movie, on the other hand, nothing tangible has changed in our lives. We are not required to alter the course of our actions in any way as a result of how the story was resolved.

And so, how is it that we can enjoy one activity that is inherently passive and irrelevant, and loathe another that is interactive and relevant? Because screenwriters and directors figured out long ago that if you avoid nurturing conflict in your story, no one will want to watch your movie. And they also figured out that it is during the first ten minutes that they must use drama to hook their viewers, so that they are willing to stay engaged for another two hours.

THE HOOK

The key to injecting drama into a meeting lies in setting up the plot from the outset. Participants need to be jolted a little during the first ten minutes of a meeting, so that they understand and appreciate what is at stake.

This might call for the leader to illustrate the dangers of making a bad decision, or highlight a competitive threat that is looming. It can also be accomplished by appealing to participants' commitment to the larger mission of the organization, and its impact on clients, employees, or society at large. If this sounds far-fetched or contrived, consider the following example:

A leader kicking off a meeting about controlling expenses:

Typical opening scene: "Alright, people, we are 12 percent over budget, and from what I can tell, we're spending way too much money on travel. Going forward, we need to have better controls and monitoring so we can meet the corporate guidelines laid out in the budget. . . . "

More dramatic opening scene: "Okay, everyone, we're here to talk about cutting expenses, which doesn't sound like much fun. But consider that there are plenty of people out there who have a vested interest in the way we spend our money. Our competitors are hoping we throw our money around carelessly. And they're certainly looking for ways to reduce their own unnecessary expenses. Our customers don't want to have to pay higher prices for our products to cover our lack of discipline. Our families would rather see more money in our paychecks than in our travel and entertainment budget. So let's dive into this issue with a sense of urgency and focus, because I certainly want to make sure that we're using the resources in the way our investors and shareholders intended. . . . "

Employees aren't expecting Hamlet, but they're certainly looking for a reason to care. And that's what the leader of a meeting should be giving them.

Ironically, most leaders of meetings go out of their way to eliminate or minimize drama and avoid the healthy conflict that results from it. Which only drains the interest of employees.

So, am I advocating the provocation of drama and confrontation among team members to create interest during meetings? Actually, yes. And I'm encouraging leaders of meetings, as well as participants, to be miners of conflict.

MINING FOR CONFLICT

When a group of intelligent people come together to talk about issues that matter, it is both natural and productive for disagreement to occur. Resolving those issues is what makes a meeting productive, engaging, even fun.

Avoiding the issues that merit debate and disagreement not only makes the meeting boring, it guarantees that the issues won't be resolved. And this is a recipe for frustration. Ironically, that frustration often manifests itself later in the form of unproductive personal conflict, or politics.

And so a leader of a meeting must make it a priority to seek out and uncover any important issues about which team members do not agree. And when team members don't want to engage in those discussions, the leader must force them to do so. Even when it makes him or her temporarily unpopular.

When I am working with executives and their teams, I force myself to mine for conflict whenever I can. When I do, it is almost a certainty that many of the executives will come to me afterward and say something to the effect of, "Thank you for making us confront that issue. Our meetings were getting so uncomfortable because we were avoiding it, and everyone knew it was a problem."

The truth is, the only thing more painful than confronting an uncomfortable topic is pretending it doesn't exist. And I believe far more suffering is caused by failing to deal with an issue directly—and whispering about it in the hallways—than by putting it on the table and wrestling with it head on.

Of course, getting people to engage in conflict when they aren't accustomed to it is a challenge. I have found one simple method to be particularly helpful in making this easier.

REAL-TIME PERMISSION

After a leader announces to a team that more conflict will be expected from them—and it is critical that this is made clear—there will be a key moment when team members take their first risks in engaging one another in active debate. And no matter how much we prepare them for this, it is going to feel uncomfortable.

When this happens, a leader can minimize the discomfort and maximize the likelihood that conflict will continue by interrupting the participants and reminding them that what they are doing is good. As simple, even paternal, as this may seem, it is remarkably effective.

It is probably worth presenting a glimpse of how this might work, using the characters from the fable:

Connor presents his advertising plans for the coming year.

Afterward, Sophia takes a risk and announces to Connor, "I'm not sure I'm on board with your new advertising proposal." Immediately, she is a little tense.

As is Connor. "Okay. What are your concerns?"

"Well, I don't think it fits with the branding we discussed last month, and I'm afraid it's going to confuse customers."

Connor is now a little frustrated. "Well, the firm that handled our branding reviewed the ads last week, and they didn't seem to have a problem with them."

Sophia turns just a little red. "Well, maybe they didn't pay close enough attention. Or maybe they're not very familiar with our customers."

Connor sighs. Before he responds, Casey interrupts. "Before you continue, and I definitely want you to continue, I just want to say that this is *exactly* the kind of thing I was talking about when I said we need to start engaging in more conflict. And even though it can be frustrating for you, Connor, to have to rethink the work you've been doing, it's Sophia's job, and all of ours, to question you if we think it can make the final outcome better."

Based on my experience, the impact of Casey's remarks would be the following:

Connor and Sophia would let go of a considerable amount of the unnecessary interpersonal tension they had been feeling.

This would allow them to retain their ideological passion around the issue, and continue to advocate their positions without being distracted or discouraged by their fears of personal rejection.

Unfortunately, even if leaders of meetings learned to master the art of producing and directing terrifically dramatic meetings filled with compelling and engaging conflict, they would still fail if that's all they did. That's because there is another big problem with meetings.

PROBLEM #2: LACK OF CONTEXTUAL STRUCTURE

No matter what kind of organizations I work with—regardless of size, industry, or geography—the same general experience drives people crazy when it comes to meetings. Here is a typical example:

Let's say the meeting in question is a standard Monday morning staff meeting, scheduled to go from 9 to 11 A.M. The leader prepares an agenda, which is basically a list of five or six items that he sends to everyone, asking for their reactions, comments, or additions. Of course, he receives none.

The meeting begins at approximately nine o'clock, with the first item on the agenda (but not necessarily the most important one). This topic occupies the first long hour of the meeting because people know that they're going to be there for the whole time, so they find *something* to say.

The second topic (again, not necessarily the second most important one) then soaks up another forty-five minutes. This leaves fifteen minutes for the final three topics (which, again, may or may not be the most important ones), not to mention any other administrative, tactical, or strategic issues that someone inevitably decides needs to be discussed.

The meeting adjourns at 11:20, with everyone frustrated for different reasons:

One team member is peeved that the meeting went overtime, again, because it means she is now late for her next meeting, and that's going to set her entire day back.

Another is upset that his issue didn't get put on the table until the end of the meeting, when there was little time and even less interest remaining.

Still another believes that the meeting was too administrative, with no focus on the important strategic issues like competitive positioning and branding . . . while the one sitting across from her actually thought that there was too *much* brainstorming, and not enough time focused on solving immediate, tactical problems like expense controls and vacation policies.

Finally, one member of the team is upset because, once again, they failed to set a final date for the company picnic.

And the leader walks away bloodied by the dissatisfaction of the team, and dumbfounded that so many people could be so unhappy about so many different things. He vows that the next meeting will be more practical, more strategic, shorter, and yes, a date will be set for the picnic.

This may not be exactly like meetings in your organization. But it represents many of the problems that I encounter time and time again in the companies that I observe. All of these problems amount to one big mess that I call "meeting stew."

MEETING STEW

The single biggest structural problem facing leaders of meetings is the tendency to throw every type of issue that needs to be discussed into the same meeting, like a bad stew with too many random ingredients. Desperate to minimize wasted time, leaders decide that they will have one big staff meeting, either once a week or every other week. They sit down in a room for two or three or four hours and hash *everything* out—sales strategies, expense policies, potential mergers, employee recognition programs, budgets, and branding—so that everyone can get back to their "real work."

Unfortunately, this only ensures that the meeting will be ineffective and unsatisfying for everyone. Why? Because some people want the meeting to be informative and quick, an efficient exchange of data and tactical information. Others think it should be interactive and strategic, providing key analysis and data to make critical decisions. Others would like to step back, take a breath, and talk meaningfully about company culture and people. Others just want to make clear decisions and move on. Who's right? Everyone. And that's the point.

THE FOUR MEETINGS

There should be different meetings for different purposes, and each of them serves a valid and important function. I propose that every organization consider adopting something like the following structure, which involves four basic types of meetings.

Meeting #1: The Daily Check-In

I hesitate to start with this one, because it is not necessarily practical for every organization. But for those that can make it work, the Daily Check-in is powerful. And even for those that can't, it is helpful to understand its rationale.

The Daily Check-in is something that I adopted and adapted from a friend of mine, Verne Harnish, who wrote a great book called *Mastering the Rockefeller Habits* in which he refers to a similar type of meeting as a "huddle." The Daily Check-in requires that team members get together, standing up, for about five minutes every morning to report on their activities that day. Five minutes. Standing up. That's it.

The purpose of the Daily Check-in is to help team members avoid confusion about how priorities are translated into action on a regular basis. It provides a quick forum for ensuring that nothing falls through the cracks on a given day and that no one steps on anyone else's toes. Just as important, it helps eliminate the need for unnecessary and time-consuming e-mail chains about schedule coordination.

Now, the Daily Check-in can be impractical for many organizations where team members work in different locations and time zones. And while a check-in can be done by phone, it isn't always wise to go to great lengths to make them happen in an organization where it is just not feasible. Still, though not indispensable for every team, the Daily Check-in can be a valuable tool for many organizations who want to better align their executives.

Inevitable Challenges

One of the certain challenges in making the Daily Check-in work will be getting team members to *stick with it initially,* long enough to make it part of their routine. It will be all too easy for busy team members to lobby for abandoning the Daily Check-in before they have given it a chance.

The key to overcoming this is to keep these meetings consistent in terms of where and when they occur. Additionally, it will be extremely important not to cancel any, even if only two members of the team are in the office on a given day.

A more common challenge with the Daily Check-in will be *keeping it to five minutes.* If the meetings exceed their time limit slightly because team members are socializing a little, that's actually okay. But if they're going long because team members are trying to address issues every morning that should be discussed at the Weekly Tactical, this is a problem. What will ultimately happen is that people will get tired of having what feels like a daily staff meeting.

One way to avoid this is to prohibit people from sitting down during Daily Check-ins. More important, the team must be disciplined, even unreasonably so, about ending the sessions after no more than ten minutes.

Finally, to avoid both of these likely obstacles, teams should commit to doing Daily Check-ins for a set period of time—perhaps two months—before evaluating whether or not they are working

Meeting #2: The Weekly Tactical

Every team needs to have regular meetings focused exclusively on tactical issues of immediate concern. Whether it takes place weekly or every other week doesn't really matter. What does matter is that everyone always attends, and that it is run with a sense of discipline and structural consistency.

A Weekly Tactical meeting should last between forty-five and ninety minutes, depending on its frequency, and should include a few critical elements, including the following:

The Lightning Round

This is a quick, around-the-table reporting session in which everyone indicates their two or three priorities for the week. It should take each team member no more than one minute (yes, sixty seconds!) to quickly describe what is on their respective plates. So even a large team should be able to accomplish this in ten minutes or so.

The lightning round is critical because it sets the tone for the rest of the meeting. By giving all participants a real sense of the actual activities taking place in the organization, it makes it easy for the team to identify potential redundancies, gaps, or other issues that require immediate attention.

Progress Review

The next key ingredient for the Weekly Tactical meeting is the routine reporting of critical information or metrics: revenue, expenses, customer satisfaction, inventory, and the like. What is reported depends on the particular industry and organizational situation, of course. The point here is to get into the habit of reviewing progress relating to key metrics for success, but not every metric available. Four or six, maybe. This should take no more than five minutes, even when allowing for quick questions for clarification of numbers. Lengthy discussion of underlying issues, on the other hand, should be avoided here.

Real-Time Agenda

Once the lightning round and progress review are complete (usually no more than fifteen minutes into the meeting), now it is time to talk about the agenda. That's right. Counter to conventional wisdom about meetings, the agenda for a weekly tactical should *not* be set before the meeting, but only after the lightning round and regular reporting activities have taken place.

This makes sense because the agenda should be based on what everyone is actually working on and how the company is performing against its goals, not based on the leader's best guess forty-eight hours prior to the meeting. Trying to predict the right priorities before these critical pieces of information are reviewed is unwise.

Leaders of meetings must therefore have something I call *disciplined spontaneity,* which means they must avoid the temptation to prepare an agenda ahead of time, and instead allow it to take shape during the meeting itself. While this might mean sacrificing some control, it ensures that the meeting will be relevant and effective.

Settling on the real-time agenda isn't terribly hard because the important topics will be easy to identify by that point. Inevitably, a few issues that need to be discussed will jump out: "Should we increase advertising this month to jump-start sales?" "Should Marketing or Business Development talk to analysts about our product issues?" "Should we freeze hiring or accelerate it?" "What are we going to do about the spending overruns?" That kind of stuff. Tactical issues that must be addressed to ensure that short-term objectives are not in jeopardy.

During the Weekly Tactical, there are two overriding goals: resolution of issues and reinforcement of clarity. Obstacles need to be identified and removed, and everyone needs to be on the same page.

Inevitable Challenges

A number of likely obstacles can prevent the proper implementation of Weekly Tactical meetings.

One of them is *the temptation to set an agenda ahead of time,* either formally or informally. While this is understandable given conventional wisdom, it is not wise. That's because it is critical for team members to come to the Weekly Tactical with an open mind, and to let the real activities and progress against objectives determine what needs to be discussed.

Another common problem is the tendency of team members to go into *too much detail during the lightning round.* This causes others to lose interest, which clouds the ability of the team to identify the right issues for discussion and resolution. The key to avoiding this challenge is to hold team members to sixty seconds during the lightning round, which is plenty of time to provide a quick summary of key activities, and even answer a question or two for clarification. If this is difficult to believe, stare at a clock for sixty seconds. You'll realize that it is a lot longer period of time than it seems, and that a lot of information can be relayed during it.

While these are both important problems to be aware of, by far the most common and dangerous challenge in making Weekly Tacticals work is the temptation to get into *discussions about long-term strategic issues.* Why is this such an important problem to avoid?

First, there isn't enough time during a Weekly Tactical to properly discuss major issues. Important, complex topics deserve enough time for brainstorming, analysis, even preparation. Moreover, even the best executives don't easily shift back and forth between topics of different magnitude, like deciding whether to change the policy on business class air travel and whether to merge with a competitor. It is the equivalent of a husband and wife trying to discuss what to do about their child's discipline problem in the same breath as deciding what to have for dinner.

A final problem with mixing strategic and tactical topics during meetings has to do with the tendency of leaders to inappropriately reconsider strategic decisions when faced with inevitable tactical obstacles. Limiting Weekly Tactical meetings to specific, short-term topics requires people to focus on solving problems, rather than backing off of long-term decisions that have already been made.

The key to overcoming this challenge is discipline. When strategic issues are raised—and they will inevitably be raised—it is critical for the leader to take them off the table and put them on a list of possible topics to be discussed during a different meeting: the Monthly Strategic.

Meeting #3: The Monthly Strategic

This is the most interesting and in many ways the most important type of meeting any team has. It is also the most fun. It is where executives wrestle with, analyze, debate, and decide upon critical issues (but only a few) that will affect the business in fundamental ways. Monthly Strategic meetings allow executives to dive into a given topic or two without the distractions of deadlines and tactical concerns.

The length of a Monthly Strategic will vary depending on the topic or topics being considered. However, it is advisable to schedule at least two hours per topic so that participants feel comfortable engaging in open-ended conversation and debate.

Whether teams decide to have these meetings once a month or every two weeks is not really important. What is important is that these strategic meetings occur regularly so that they can serve as a timely "parking lot" for critical strategic issues that come up during the Weekly Tactical meetings. This gives executives the confidence to table critical issues, knowing they will eventually be addressed.

Ad Hoc Strategic Meetings

In some cases, a strategic or critical issue that gets raised in a Weekly Tactical meeting cannot wait for the next Monthly Strategic meeting on the schedule. Still, that doesn't mean it should be taken up during that Weekly Tactical.

Instead, executives should create an ad hoc meeting specifically for the purpose of taking on that issue. It should be clearly separated from the Weekly Tactical so that executives can reset their minds to the nature of the meeting, and so enough time can be allotted for appropriate analysis and discussion. If all this requires that executives clear their schedules later that day or stay into the evening, then so be it. If the issue is truly critical, then it is worth such a sacrifice.

In many ways, this Ad Hoc Strategic meeting is the most important one that occurs in an organization. It demonstrates that an executive team knows how to identify those rare strategic issues that deserve immediate attention even at the expense of the urgent but less important tactical concerns that surface every day. Great organizations rally around these issues with the kind of focus and urgency that allow them to outmaneuver competitors who are too mired in the monotony of their meetings, or who wait for a full-blown crisis before rallying around an important topic.

If these strategic meetings can take place whenever an issue warrants them, then why did I call them *Monthly* Strategics? Because if we do not schedule regular meetings to talk about important topics, we will find ourselves looking back after four months and wondering why we haven't had any strategic conversations at all. Choosing a regular interval is an important step to ensuring that strategic meetings don't fall by the wayside.

Inevitable Challenges

The most obvious challenge in implementing Monthly Strategic meetings (or the ad hoc variety) is the *failure to schedule enough time* for them. In the heat of daily schedules and demands on executives' time, the idea of carving out three or four hours for one or two issues is harder than it seems in theory. But it is critical. Sometimes it takes forty-five minutes of discussion at the beginning of a Monthly Strategic just to unearth the real underlying issue at the heart of a problem.

A related challenge has to do with *putting too many items on the agenda*. This is an understandable temptation for executives who want to discuss every important issue. Unfortunately, it only dilutes the quality of the debate around the most critical ones.

The key to avoiding both of these challenges is to ensure that more than enough time is scheduled for each issue. That means if there are three issues to resolve, the meeting needs to be much longer than if there is only one. Again, if that means clearing everyone's calendars for an entire day, so be it.

In my work, I have found that most executives have far too many tactical and administrative items on their schedules, which is often the result of an adrenaline addiction, the need to stay occupied with moment-to-moment activities. And so they initially resist taking an entire day for meetings to discuss strategy, because they fear falling behind in their daily adrenal activities. However, once they force themselves to carve out time for strategic conversations, they almost always are glad they did, and they are surprised that they didn't really miss anything critical by being away from their desks for the afternoon.

Another challenge in making strategic meetings work is *the failure to do research and preparation* ahead of time. The quality of a strategic discussion, and the decision that results from it, are improved greatly by a little preliminary work. This eliminates the all-too-common reliance on anecdotal decision making. The key to ensuring that preparation occurs is to let team members know as far in advance as possible what issues will be discussed during the Monthly or Ad Hoc Strategic. Of course, the leader must also hold team members accountable for coming to the meetings prepared.

Finally, I would be remiss if I didn't mention a final challenge: *the fear of conflict.* Monthly and Ad Hoc Strategic meetings cannot be effective unless there is a willingness on the part of team members to engage in unfiltered, productive ideological debate. This also applies to the final type of meeting: the Quarterly Off-Site Review.

Meeting #4: The Quarterly Off-Site Review

The executive off-site has earned a reputation as a time-wasting, touchy-feely boondoggle, and in many cases, rightly so. Whether executives are golfing, catching each other falling out of trees, or exploring their collective inner child, many off-site meetings contribute little lasting benefit to an organization.

This is a shame, not only because of the time, money, and credibility that are sacrificed, but because of the critical role that off-site meetings should play in the context of all the other meetings that serve the organization.

Topics to Cover

Effective off-sites provide executives an opportunity to regularly step away from the daily, weekly, even monthly issues that occupy their attention, so they can review the business in a more holistic, long-term manner. Topics for reflection and discussion at a productive Quarterly Off-Site Review might include the following:

- *Comprehensive Strategy Review:* Executives should reassess their strategic direction, not every day as so many do, but three or four times a year. Industries change and new competitive threats emerge that call for different approaches. Reviewing strategies annually or semiannually is usually not often enough to stay current.

- *Team Review:* Executives should regularly assess themselves and their behaviors as a team, identifying trends or tendencies that may not be serving the organization. This often requires a change of scenery so that executives can interact with one another on a more personal level and remind themselves of their collective commitments to the team.
- *Personnel Review:* Three or four times a year, executives should talk, across departments, about the key employees within the organization. Every member of an executive team should know whom their peers view as their stars, as well as their poor performers. This allows executives to provide perspectives that might actually alter those perceptions based on different experiences and points of view. More important, it allows them to jointly manage and retain top performers, and work with poor performers similarly.
- *Competitive and Industry Review:* Information about competitors and industry trends bleeds into an organization little by little over time. It is useful for executives to step back and look at what is happening around them in a more comprehensive way so they can spot trends that individual nuggets of information might not make clear. Even the best executives can lose sight of the forest for the trees when inundated with daily responsibilities.

Inevitable Challenges

A variety of challenges can prevent a team from correctly establishing effective Quarterly Off-Site Reviews. None are particularly dangerous by themselves, but together they can hinder the effectiveness of these important meetings, and ultimately, lead to their demise.

One of the challenges is *the tendency to overburden and over-structure the meetings,* which usually takes the form of tightly scheduled slide presentations and lengthy informational sermons. The purpose of a Quarterly Off-Site Review is to reflect on and discuss the state of the organization, not to provide executives with presentations and white papers.

Another challenge is the temptation to make these meetings *too much of a boondoggle* by having them at exotic locations that require extensive travel, and by including too many social activities. The purpose of getting out of the office is not to entertain the attendees, but rather to allow them to step back from daily distractions and interruptions. As a result, driving an hour away to a comfortable hotel or conference center is usually enough to do the trick. Flying to Aruba or Hawaii does not eliminate distractions, it merely substitutes one type (e.g. snorkeling and golf) for another (e.g. work interruptions).

Another interesting problem is *inviting outsiders to attend* the meeting, in the spirit of inclusivity. While this may be tempting for a variety of reasons (e.g. more input, or involvement and exposure for employees), it is a very bad idea for exactly one: it changes the team dynamic. Adding even one employee who is not a member of the team, no matter how well liked or well informed that person is, can negate one of the most important reasons for having off-sites: improving team unity.

The only exception to this rule might be the use of an outside facilitator, someone who is trusted by the team, understands the organization's business, and is driven to help the team accomplish its objectives, not his or her own objectives. The greatest benefit of using such a facilitator is that it allows the leader of the team to participate fully in the discussions without having to worry about playing a more objective, supporting role.

(Please note: The chart on the following page differs slightly from Will's White Board in the fable because it is not based on comparisons to film and television.)

The Four Meetings

Meeting Type	Time Required	Purpose and Format	Keys to Success
Daily Check-in	5 minutes	Share daily schedules and activities.	• Don't sit down. • Keep it administrative. • Don't cancel even when some people can't be there.
Weekly Tactical	45–90 minutes	Review weekly activities and metrics, and resolve tactical obstacles and issues.	• Don't set agenda until after initial reporting. • Postpone strategic discussions.
Monthly Strategic (or Ad Hoc Strategic)	2–4 hours	Discuss, analyze, brainstorm, and decide upon critical issues affecting long-term success.	• Limit to one or two topics. • Prepare and do research. • Engage in good conflict.
Quarterly Off-site Review	1–2 days	Review strategy, industry trends, competitive landscape, key personnel, team development.	• Get out of office. • Focus on work; limit social activities. • Don't overstructure or overburden the schedule.

THE BIGGEST CHALLENGE OF ALL: "THE MYTH OF TOO MANY MEETINGS"

Most of my friends reacted the same way when they heard that I was writing a book called *Death by Meeting*. As you may have done, they assumed I was going to make a case for having fewer meetings.

And so, upon hearing about Daily Check-ins, Weekly Tacticals, Monthly Strategics, and Quarterly Off-Site Reviews, you might be thinking, "This is crazy. Where am I going to find the time to do all this? I'm already going to too many meetings."

While it is true that much of the time we currently spend in meetings is largely wasted, the solution is not to stop having meetings, but rather to make them better. Because when properly utilized, meetings are actually time *savers*.

That's right. Good meetings provide opportunities to improve execution by accelerating decision making and eliminating the need to revisit issues again and again. But they also produce a subtle but enormous benefit by reducing unnecessarily repetitive motion and communication in the organization. The reason that we don't see this upon first glance is that we fail to account for something that I like to call "sneaker time."

SNEAKER TIME

Most executives I know spend hours sending e-mail, leaving voice mail, and roaming the halls to clarify issues that should have been made clear during a meeting in the first place. But no one accounts for this the way they do when they add up time spent in meetings.

I have no doubt that sneaker time is the most subtle, dangerous, and underestimated black hole in corporate America. To understand it, it is helpful to take a quick look at the basic geometry of an executive team within the context of an organization.

Consider that an executive team with just seven people has twenty-one combinations of one-to-one relationships that have to be maintained in order to keep people on the same page. That alone is next to impossible for a human being to track.

But when you consider the dozens of employees down throughout the organization who report to those seven and who need to be on the same page with one another, the communication challenge increases dramatically, as does the potential for wasting time and energy. And so, when we fail to get clarity and alignment during meetings, we set in motion a colossal wave of human activity as executives and their direct reports scramble to figure out what everyone else is doing and why.

Remarkably, because sneaker time is mixed in with everything else we do during the day, we fail to see it as a single category of wasted time. It never ceases to amaze me when I see executives checking their watches at the end of a meeting and lobbying the CEO for it to end so they can "go do some real work." In so many cases, the "real work" they're referring to is going back to their offices to respond to e-mail and voice mail that they've received only because so many people are confused about what needs to be done.

It's as if the executives are saying, "Can we wrap this up so I can run around and explain to people what I never explained to them after the last meeting?" It is at once shocking and understandable that intelligent people cannot see the correlation between failing to take the time to get clarity, closure, and buy-in during a meeting, and the time required to clean up after themselves as a result.

A FINAL THOUGHT ON MEETINGS

Just as the cover of this book suggests, bad meetings exact a toll on the human beings who must endure them, and this goes far beyond mere momentary dissatisfaction. Bad meetings, and what they indicate and provoke in an organization, generate real human suffering in the form of anger, lethargy, and cynicism. And while this certainly has a profound impact on organizational life, it also impacts people's self-esteem, their families, and their outlook on life.

And so, for those of us who lead organizations and the employees who work within them, improving meetings is not just an opportunity to enhance the performance of our companies. It is also a way to positively impact the lives of our people. And that includes us.

Below is a simple form that may be helpful in managing your Weekly Tactical meetings.

Weekly Tactical Meeting Guide

Date: ____________

I. Lightning Round Notes

II. Key Metrics Review

Goal/Metric	Behind	On Target	Ahead	Unknown
1. ____________	☐	☐	☐	☐
2. ____________	☐	☐	☐	☐
3. ____________	☐	☐	☐	☐
4. ____________	☐	☐	☐	☐
5. ____________	☐	☐	☐	☐

III. Tactical Agenda Items

Order	Topic
___	____________
___	____________
___	____________
___	____________
___	____________
___	____________

IV. Potential Strategic Topics

Topic

____

____

____

____

____

____

V. Decisions/Actions

VI. Cascading Messages

ACKNOWLEDGMENTS

So many people to thank.

First, I thank my wife, Laura, for your integrity and passion and principle. And for the loving sacrifices you make for me and our boys every day, which are far more important than anything I do. And to those three boys, Connor, Matthew, and Casey, thank you for making me giddy with joy every single day, and for coming to visit me at the hotel to make my writing less lonely.

And I thank my humble and hungry staff at The Table Group. Your talent, commitment, and friendship mean more to me with every year we spend together. Thanks to Tracy Noble for keeping me on track with this book, and for your astounding attention to detail and quality. To Amy Hiett for every selfless thing you've done over the years, which is impossible to fully comprehend, to make me and our company work. To Jeff Gibson for carrying the water while I was writing, and for your capacity to tolerate and learn from the rest of us. To Karen Amador for all of the little things you do that are so very big and gracefully done. To Michele Rango for your fearlessness and passion. And to Amber Hunter, for your persistence and dedication. And thanks to all of your families for letting me play with you every day.

Of course, I thank my parents, for all of the obvious biological-historical-financial reasons. And for your complete and untiring support now and over the years. And to Ritamarie and Mark Tennyson and Vince and Nora Lencioni, for your love and support from near and far.

I thank my editor, Susan Williams, for your steadiness, insights, and trust, all of which I appreciate more with each book. And to everyone else at Jossey-Bass and Wiley, Erik Thrasher, Todd Berman, Jesica Church, Rob Brandt, Jeff Wyneken, Deborah Hunter, Cedric Crocker, Rob Dyer, Rick Gresh, Dean Karrel, Will Pesce, and so many others. Thanks for your commitment to me and these ideas.

I thank my agent, Jim Levine, for your counsel and genuine concern for me and our firm.

I thank Charlotte Rogers for keeping the boys safe, and Laura and me sane.

I thank all of the special "readers" who gave me insightful and substantive feedback in a pinch: John Rodriguez, Susan and John Beans, Jean Kovacs, Mark Weidick and Rick Schultz. And I thank my friends who don't hear from me or see me for months at a time while I am writing: the Beans, the Carlsons, the Garners, the Bellis, the Bolles, the Patchs, the Elys, the Berrys, the Gilmores, the Grubers, the Fraziers, the Hammits, the Groningers, the Robles, and so many others who probably won't call me back.

I thank all of the clients that have given me and my colleagues the privilege to work in their organizations and speak to their employees over these past few years. I cannot tell you how much I appreciate your trust and passion and generosity. I wish I could name you all individually.

I thank the organizations that have befriended The Table Group: the Alliance of Chief Executives, Solutions@Work, TEC, the Young Entrepreneurs' Organization, the Young Presidents' Organization, and others. And I thank Verne Harnish and Gazelles, Inc., for your support and advice over the years.

I thank all of the many, many teachers, coaches, managers, and mentors who have contributed to my development over the years. I thank the community at St. Isidore Church and School for making such a difference for my family. And I thank everyone at the Make-A-Wish Foundation for the wonderful work you do, and for allowing me to play a small part in that for the past few years.

And finally, for bringing all of these people into my life, and for giving us everything that is good, I thank You, Lord.

ABOUT THE AUTHOR

Patrick Lencioni is founder and president of The Table Group, a management consulting firm specializing in executive team development and organizational health. As a consultant and keynote speaker, he has worked with thousands of senior executives in organizations ranging from Fortune 500s and high-tech start-ups to universities and nonprofits. Clients who have engaged his services include New York Life, Southwest Airlines, Sam's Club, Microsoft, Allstate, Visa, FedEx, and the U.S. Military Academy, West Point, to name a few. He is the author of five nationally recognized books, including the *New York Times* best-seller *The Five Dysfunctions of a Team* (Jossey-Bass, 2002).

Patrick lives in the San Francisco Bay Area with his wife, Laura, and their three sons, Matthew, Connor, and Casey.

To learn more about Patrick and The Table Group, please visit www.tablegroup.com.

To learn more about Patrick Lencioni and his other products and services, including free resources and his newsletter, please visit **www.tablegroup.com**

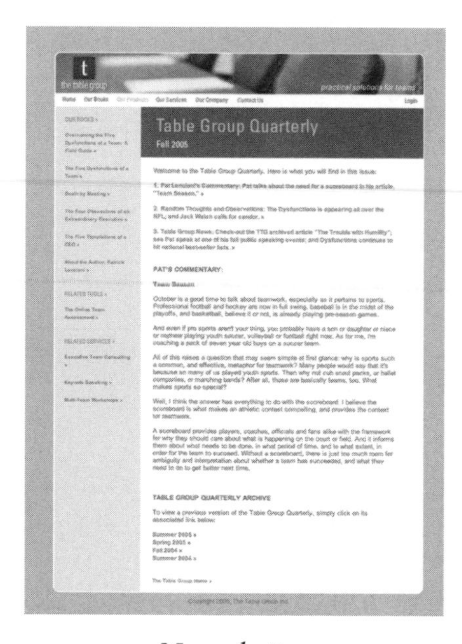

Newsletter

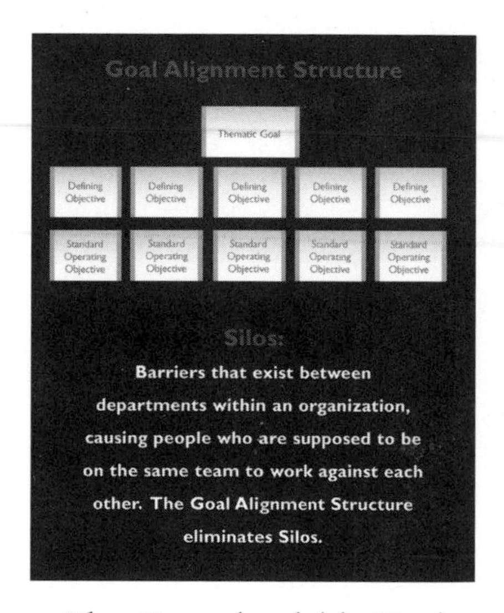

Silos Downloadable Tool